THE ROUGH GUIDE TO
Clarinet

**Whether you're a beginner or a pro,
whether you are about to buy a clarinet
or you want to learn more about the one
you already have – this book is for you.**

Hugo Pinksterboer

THE ESSENTIAL TIPBOOK

Publishing Details

This first edition published Nov 2001 by Rough Guides Ltd,
62–70 Shorts Gardens, London WC2H 9AH
Distributed by the Penguin Group:
Penguin Books Ltd, 27 Wrights Lane, London W8 5TZ
Typeset in Glasgow and Minion to an original design by
The Tipbook Company bv
Printed in The Netherlands by Hentenaar Boek bv, Nieuwegein
No part of this book may be reproduced in any form without
permission from the publisher except for the quotation of brief
passages in reviews.
The publishers and authors have done their best to ensure the
accuracy and currency of all the information in The Rough Guide,
however, they can accept no responsibility for any loss, injury or
inconvenience sustained as a result of information or advice
contained in the guide. Trademarks and/or usernames have been
used in this book solely to identify the products or instruments
discussed. Such use does not identify endorsement by or
affiliation with the trademark owner(s).
©The Tipbook Company bv, 2001
152 pp
A catalogue record for this book is available from the British
Library.
1-85828-753-7

THE ROUGH GUIDE TO
Clarinet

Written by

Hugo Pinksterboer

**ROUGH
GUIDES**

THE ESSENTIAL TIPBOOK

Rough Guide Tipbook Credits

Journalist, writer and musician **Hugo Pinksterboer** has written hundreds of articles and reviews for international music magazines. He is the author of the reference work for cymbals (*The Cymbal Book*, Hal Leonard, US) and has written and developed a wide variety of musical manuals and courses.

Illustrator, designer and musician **Gijs Bierenbroodspot** has worked as an art director in magazines and advertising. While searching in vain for information about saxophone mouthpieces he came up with the idea for this series of books on music and musical instruments. Since then, he has created the layout and the illustrations for all of the books.

Acknowledgements

Concept, design and illustrations: Gijs Bierenbroodspot

Translation: MdJ Copy & Translation

Editors: Andrew Dickson and Duncan Clark

IN BRIEF

Have you just started to play the clarinet? Are you thinking about buying an instrument, or do you just want to know more about the one you already own? If so, this book will tell you all you need to know. You'll read about buying or renting a clarinet; about wooden and plastic instruments; about bores and barrels, toneholes, reeds and mouthpieces; about tuning and maintenance; about the clarinet's history and the members of the clarinet family. And much more besides.

Getting the most from your clarinet

Once you've read this book you'll be in a good position to get the best from your clarinet, and to make a good choice when you go out to buy an instrument. You'll also understand all the jargon you're likely to come across if you read more about the clarinet in books, magazines and brochures, or on the Internet.

Begin at the beginning

If you've only just started playing or haven't yet begun, pay special attention to the first four chapters. If you've been playing for longer, you may prefer to skip ahead to Chapter 5.

Glossary

Most of the clarinet terms you'll come across in this book are briefly explained in the glossary at the end, which doubles as an index.

CONTENTS

1. THE CLARINET

As a clarinettist you can join all kinds of groups and orchestras, and play many different styles of music – from classical to modern, folk to jazz and much more. This chapter introduces the instrument: what you can do with it, how it sounds and the various shapes and sizes of clarinet you may come across.

One of the most unusual things about the clarinet is its versatility. It can be played so soft as to be almost inaudible, yet loudly enough to be heard above an entire orchestra. It can sound incredibly deep, or very high. And you can make it sound shy and coy – or, just as easily, strident and brash.

A good blend

You hear clarinettists playing so many different styles of music because clarinets 'blend' well with all kinds of instruments. A clarinet sounds at home with the violins in a symphony orchestra, with the trumpets in a concert band, or with other clarinets in a *clarinet choir*.

Other groups

And those are only a few examples. Clarinets also sound excellent in combination with a piano or a human voice, and in a chamber group like a wind quintet (along with flute, oboe, bassoon and French horn). And then there's jazz: nearly all old-style jazz bands feature a clarinettist, and some modern groups do too. In Chapter 15 you can read more about the different kinds of groups and orchestras you can join as a clarinettist.

How you sound

For classical music, clarinettists usually want their instruments to sound dark and warm. Clarinettists who play outdoors usually want a louder, 'bigger' sound. And jazz players often look for a brighter, more flexible sound. All of them are possible, and you can largely determine the sound yourself: what your instrument sounds like has a great deal to do with how you play it.

Learning to play

Learning to play the clarinet is not too hard – to start with, anyway. With half an hour's practice a day you'll be able to play a few simple tunes in a matter of weeks. What takes much longer is learning to get a beautiful sound from your clarinet and to control your tuning properly.

Shapes . . .

Clarinets come in a few different shapes and many different sizes. They can be made of wood or plastic, they can be almost black but they also come in bright colours. And they use all kinds of different mechanisms. All of these differences are discussed in this book.

. . . and sizes

As well as the 'ordinary' clarinet that most clarinettists play, there are many other types. The bass clarinet, shown in the drawing, is one. It's a good deal bigger,

Different shapes and sizes: a B flat clarinet and a bass clarinet

which makes it sound much deeper. But playing the bass clarinet is not quite the same as simply playing a 'big clarinet', which is why there are musicians who specialize in that instrument.

More

There are even bigger clarinets, too, and much smaller ones. In Chapter 11 you can read about the various different sizes. The biggest of all is the sub-contrabass clarinet, which is coiled up because it would otherwise be too long to play.

B flat clarinet

The 'ordinary' clarinet is officially called the *soprano clarinet in B flat* or, more usually, the *B flat clarinet*. The reason for these names will be explained in the next chapter.

Flat and sharp signs

As you'll soon learn when you start playing the clarinet, 'flat' is also written with a symbol: ♭. The opposite term, *sharp*, also has a symbol: ♯. You'll find both the words and the symbols used in this book.

2. A QUICK TOUR

With all those keys and rods, a clarinet looks much more complicated than it actually is. In this chapter you'll find out which parts make up a clarinet and what all those components are for. You'll also meet the bass clarinet and a few other members of the family.

Essentially a clarinet is a long tube with holes in it. Just as on a recorder, you play the lowest note by closing off all of those *toneholes*. If you open the last hole, the tone goes up. If you then open the next tonehole, the tone goes up some more – and so on.

Finger extensions

The toneholes of a clarinet are too far apart for you to be able to cover them all with your fingers. Besides, there are more toneholes than you have fingers. That's why the instrument has all of those levers: they act as extensions.

Five parts

A clarinet consists of five parts. Right at the top is the *mouthpiece* with the *reed*. When you play the clarinet, you blow against the reed. This makes it vibrate, and the reed in turn makes the air in the clarinet vibrate – and vibrating air is sound.

Barrel

Under the mouthpiece is the *barrel*. Since you use it to tune the clarinet, it's also known as the *tuning barrel*. In the UK, it's sometimes called the *tuning socket*, or just the *socket*.

Upper joint and lower joint

The two largest sections of the clarinet are the upper or left-hand joint, and the lower or right-hand joint.

Thumbrest

When you play, the weight of the clarinet rests on your right thumb. On many clarinets the thumbrest can be adjusted – set a little bit higher or lower – to make the fit as good as possible.

The bell

At the bottom of the lower joint is the *bell*, the widely flared end of the clarinet.

MECHANISM

The keys and *key rods* or axles are collectively called the *mechanism* or *keywork*. To start with it looks rather complicated, but it isn't really.

Your fingers

The mechanism becomes a lot easier to understand if you look only at the keys and levers your fingers rest on. Those keys and levers are the ones shown as 'solid' in the illustrations on the page opposite.

Six rings

Clarinets usually have six *ring keys* or *rings*, five of them at the front of the instrument. The sixth is at the back, by the left thumb.

Seventeen keys

Most clarinets have seventeen keys,

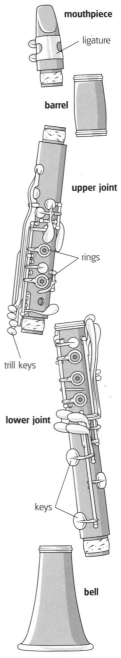

A clarinet consists of five parts

5

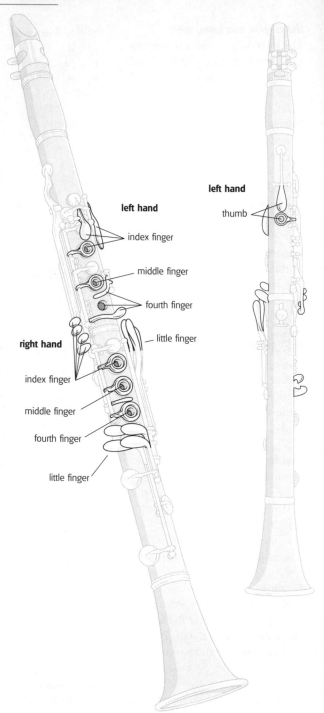

left hand

index finger

middle finger

fourth finger

right hand

little finger

index finger

middle finger

fourth finger

little finger

left hand

thumb

in addition to those six rings. These instruments are usually described as *17/6*. Other clarinets come with extra keys and rings.

Closed keys
If you have a clarinet handy, you'll be able to see that most of the keys are closed: the small keys at the top, for instance. There are springs which make sure they close again after you've opened them.

Open keys
There are only four keys which are open when you are not playing. One is right at the end of the clarinet. When you close that key along with all the others, you play the very lowest note, the low E.

Double names
You can use that lowest key to play not just the low E but also a much higher-sounding B. For that reason, this key is called the E/B key. Most of the other keys and rings are also used for at least two different notes, so they all have double names too.

Fingering chart
A fingering chart shows you exactly which keys and toneholes you must close off or *stop* to play a particular note. You can find a chart showing all the fingerings at www.tipbook.com/clarinet.

THE REGISTERS
On the back of the clarinet you'll find a special key which you operate with your left thumb. Without this *register key* you can only play twenty different notes on a clarinet.

Higher register
If you open the register key by pressing it with your left thumb, you are suddenly able to play a whole series of new, higher-sounding notes. In technical terms, you

A fingering chart showing a low B flat fingering

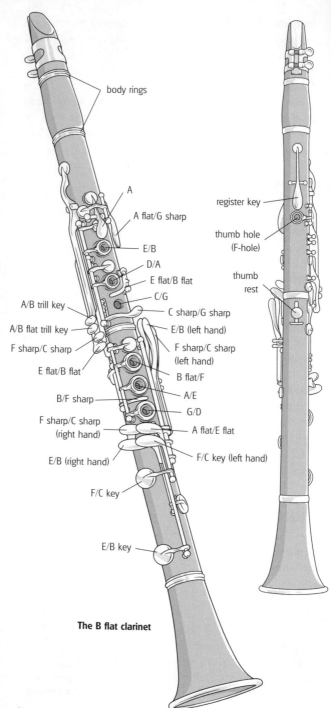

body rings

A

A flat/G sharp

E/B

D/A

E flat/B flat

C/G

A/B trill key

C sharp/G sharp

A/B flat trill key

E/B (left hand)

F sharp/C sharp

F sharp/C sharp
(left hand)

E flat/B flat

B flat/F

B/F sharp

A/E

F sharp/C sharp
(right hand)

G/D

A flat/E flat

E/B (right hand)

F/C key (left hand)

F/C key

E/B key

register key

thumb hole
(F-hole)

thumb
rest

The B flat clarinet

enter a higher *register*, which is why this key is called the register key.

Chalumeau register
When the register key is closed, what you play are the notes of the lower register. This is also known as the *chalumeau register*.

Clarinet
And with the register key open, you can play all the notes of the higher-sounding *clarinet register*, also called the *upper register*.

E and B
When you keep all the keys closed, you play the lowest note of the chalumeau register (the low E). If you then open just the register key, you hear the lowest note of the clarinet register (the B). This B sounds a lot higher.

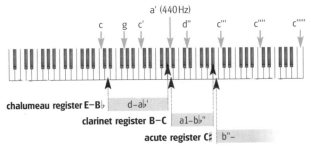

The B flat clarinet has three registers

Twelfth
On the piano keyboard above you can see that those two notes span twelve white keys. This tonal distance is called a *twelfth*, which explains why the register key is sometimes called the *twelfth key*.

Other names
Most clarinettists call the register key the *speaker key*, though it's also occasionally referred to, incorrectly, as the *octave key* (see page 114).

Higher still
On the clarinet you can play even higher than the clarinet

register – in the highest register of all, usually called the *altissimo*, *acute* or *extreme register*. It will probably take you a couple of years before you learn to play in this very high register.

MORE ABOUT KEYS

Keys have all kinds of different names too. Some clarinettists just call the E/B key the E key, for instance, while others call it the B key.

Numbers

To make things easier, the keys are sometimes numbered instead. Unfortunately, not everyone does it the same way: what one book calls key 5b is key 12 in another. So that can be confusing too.

Twice the same

Most clarinets have three keys which you can operate with either your left little finger or your right little finger. They are the keys E/B, F/C and F sharp/C sharp. This explains why those key names are shown twice on the drawing on page 8. Which little finger you use for the note will mostly depend on the notes you play just before or just after that one: which fingers you have available, in other words.

Trill keys

Your little fingers and index fingers control more than one key each. Your right index finger has no fewer than five to operate: one ring key and the four keys which you press with the 'side' of your finger. Although these side keys are commonly known as *trill keys*, only the upper two are specifically used for playing trills – though they have other jobs too.

Bridge or link

Under the trill keys you can see the *bridge* or *link*. As it connects the rings of the lower joint with the second ring of the upper joint, this mechanism is sometimes known as the *correspondence*.

Pads

Inside every *key cup* is a *pad*. This is a small disc covered

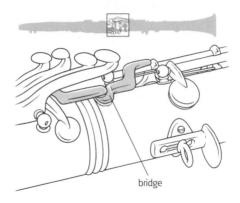

bridge

with a soft material which ensures that the key stops the tonehole properly, just as your fingertip would: without air leaking out.

Extra components

As well as the fixed components of a clarinet described above there are a few extras that you can add yourself. For instance, there are special clip-on thumb rests to make playing more comfortable (see pages 41–42). Another example is the *lyre*, a clip-on mini music stand for use in marching bands. Some lyres have a separate attachment point for a neck strap. Obviously enough, it's easier to read your part if the lyre is half way up the clarinet rather than at the end of the bell.

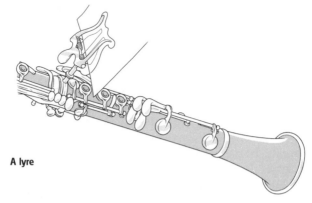

A lyre

IN B FLAT

The most common clarinet is the B flat clarinet. If you play a C on this clarinet, you actually hear a B flat, which is exactly one whole note lower than a C. Why is that?

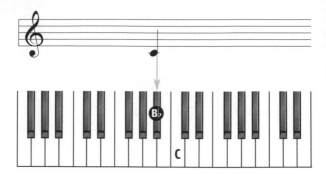

On a B flat clarinet, a written C sounds the same pitch as a B flat on the piano

Playing fingerings

If a C is shown on your score appearing on an extra line under the stave (a *ledger line*), you stop the three toneholes by your left hand. You are then playing a C *fingering*. And on a B flat clarinet that fingering gives you a *sounding B flat*, also called a *concert pitch* B flat.

C clarinets

Some clarinets are pitched in C instead. If you play a C fingering on one, it sounds a C. This seems simpler, but there is one problem: being pitched a little higher, a C clarinet is slightly shorter than a B flat clarinet. Which makes it sound just a little less warm, full and dark. This is the most important reason why just about everyone plays the B flat clarinet.

A and E flat

The clarinet in A is similar to the B flat instrument but has a slightly darker tone. Many orchestral, chamber and solo works are written for the A clarinet. In lots of orchestras, concert bands and clarinet choirs, you'll also find the small E flat clarinet, which sounds a good deal higher and brighter than the B flat clarinet. There are other clarinets in different tunings, too; they are all listed in Chapter 11.

Transposing instruments

Instruments not pitched in C are called *transposing instruments*, meaning that composers must write *transposed parts* for them. When composers want the bright sound of an E flat clarinet, for example, they write a part specially for that clarinet. If they want an E flat to sound in that part, they put down a C on the score. You play a C, the audience hears an E flat. That's all there is to it.

BASS AND ALTO CLARINETS

A bass clarinet is a lot bigger than an ordinary clarinet. In order to avoid it becoming too long, it has several bends in it: a curved, metal neck and an upward-pointing metal bell.

Closed hole keys

The toneholes which have ring keys on an ordinary clarinet are too big to stop with your fingers on a bass clarinet. That's why bass clarinets have *closed hole keys* (also called *plateau-style* or *covered keys*) for those toneholes. Bass clarinets also have more keys that you can operate with both your left and right little fingers. Otherwise the mechanism is basically the same.

In B flat

The bass clarinet is usually pitched in B flat. But if you play the same fingering as on an ordinary (soprano) B flat clarinet, the bass clarinet will sound exactly one octave lower (equal to eight white keys on a piano).

Alto clarinets

The alto clarinet, which also has a metal neck and bell, comes between the ordinary clarinet and the bass clarinet, and is pitched in E flat. Some alto clarinets have both closed hole keys and rings, others have only closed hole keys. You can find all the other types of clarinet in Chapter 11.

The alto clarinet: bigger than a B flat clarinet but smaller than a bass clarinet

13

HOW HIGH AND HOW LOW

Clarinets have a very large *range*: they can sound extremely low and also very high. Between the highest and the lowest notes there's a difference of more than three-and-a-half octaves. The range of a bass clarinet is even bigger: a good player can reach more than four octaves.

Seeing and hearing

On the piano keyboard below you can see how wide the ranges of the B flat, the alto, the bass and the E flat clarinet are.

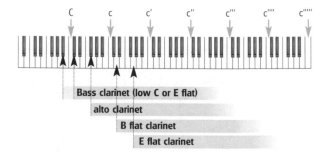

The sounding ranges of four clarinets

Several E notes

When all the keys of a clarinet are closed you play the low E. But you can also play a few higher E notes. For that reason, it's handy to be able to indicate exactly which one is meant. On the piano keyboard above you can see one way in which this is done, using capital and lowercase letters and marks. The low E on the B flat clarinet would be written as a small e. The highest E note you can play on this clarinet sounds three octaves higher: this is e'''.

French and German

This book focuses on the *French* or *Boehm clarinet*. There are also *German clarinets*, which sound and look different. They are mainly used in Germany, but you may come across them elsewhere. You can read more about them on page 50 and onwards.

3. LEARNING TO PLAY

The clarinet is not the hardest instrument to learn to play, but neither is it the easiest. You can master a few simple tunes in a matter of weeks, but you can also spend years working on your technique and tone – just like with many other instruments.

To make a clarinet sound good, you need to learn a good breathing technique. Playing the clarinet involves a lot more than simply blowing through a mouthpiece: only with good breathing can you play in tune, produce a beautiful tone and play long phrases.

Embouchure
The way your instrument sounds also has a lot to do with how you hold the mouthpiece in your mouth, how tightly you tense your lips, the position of your tongue and so on. These issues are collectively referred to as *embouchure*.

Mechanism
It doesn't usually take too long to get used to the mechanism, even if it looks complex. After all, it was devised to make a clarinet player's life as easy as possible. To start with you'll only play in the clarinet's bottom or chalumeau register (with the register key closed). After a few months to a year you'll start using the register key, which means you'll also be playing in the clarinet register. You won't get to the very highest notes for a while longer.

Too young?
The fingers of children younger than ten or eleven years

old are often still too thin to stop the toneholes or to reach all of the keys. What's more, their thumbs may not be strong enough to bear the weight of the clarinet: the instrument can easily weigh 700 to 800 grams (1½ to 1¾ pounds).

Solutions
You can make things easier with a neck strap. There are also clarinets made with mechanisms designed to fit smaller hands, and special children's clarinets are even available.

Neck straps
If you use a neck strap, the clarinet hangs around your neck rather than resting on your thumb. Straps with a broad, elastic neck band are very popular. Many clarinets have an eye which you can hook the strap into. If yours doesn't, many straps have a leather flap for attaching to the thumbrest.

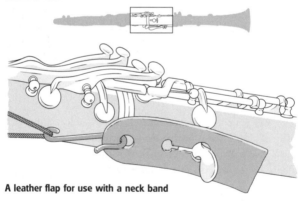

A leather flap for use with a neck band

Smaller clarinets
A neck strap won't help, though, if your fingers are too thin or too short. Some teachers might advise you to start on a smaller clarinet – such as an E flat instrument – if this is a problem for you. But there are two major drawbacks to this: you'll later have to get used to a B flat clarinet because it plays differently, and there are very few affordable E flat clarinets around. A more realistic option is to go for a clarinet on which all the rings have been replaced with plateau-style (closed hole) keys, so that you can stop the toneholes even with very small fingers.

Children's clarinets

Children aged from five or six can start off on the plastic Lyons clarinet. The instrument is pitched in C and, since the mechanism is also made of plastic, it looks very different. The Lyons has many advantages for very young players: it weighs only third of an ordinary clarinet, has extra-small toneholes, all the keys are set very close together, it needs less maintenance and is more durable. But they're not that much cheaper than a budget beginner's clarinet (see Chapter 4), so it's useful to know that these instruments are often available for rental.

Teeth

Playing the clarinet is usually no problem if you have braces on your teeth, although if you play for a long time in one go your lower brace might start giving you trouble. Playing does become difficult if you're losing your milk teeth: it may be difficult to hold the instrument steady.

A clarinet
designed
specially for
children
(Lyons)

LESSONS

If you take clarinet lessons you'll learn about everything connected with playing the clarinet: from breathing, embouchure and playing in tune to reading music and maintaining a good posture.

Private lessons

Though it's usually the most expensive option, taking lessons from a private teacher does has certain advantages. You're likely to be taught one-to-one, and be given more flexibility about how often you have lessons and how long they last.

At school

Children can usually take clarinet lessons in school. If they are subsidized, school lessons may well work out cheaper than private lessons, though often these are group lessons, with two or more pupils being taught at once.

Adults

It's never too late to start learning the clarinet. Most adults take private lessons, but you could also consider attending an adult education class.

Playing together

Most schools – and some adult education establishments – have their own ensembles or orchestras. You'll also be able to play together with other musicians if you learn to play the clarinet as a member of a music centre.

What will it cost?

How much you'll pay depends very much on the kind of tuition you go for. If you decide to have private lessons on your own, expect to pay around £10–15 for a session lasting half an hour, though of course more advanced teachers will charge more and it varies area by area. If you're having lessons from a teacher in school, they might cost from £40 per term, though again it varies depending on where you live. The best advice is to speak to the school or local education authority in question or contact a national organization such as the Clarinet & Saxophone Society of Great Britain (see page 132), who should be able to point you in the right direction.

Questions, questions

When enquiring about a teacher, don't simply find out how much the lessons cost. Here are some other questions that you may want to ask.

- Is a free **introductory lesson** included? This is a good way to find out how well you get on with the teacher, and, for that matter, with the instrument.
- Is the teacher interested in taking you on as a student if you are just doing it **for the fun of it** or are you expected to practice hours every day?
- Do you have to make a large investment in method books right away, or is **course material provided**?
- Can you **record your lessons**, so that you can listen at home to how you sound, and once more to what's been said?

- Is the teacher going to make you **practise scales** for two years, or will you be performing real pieces as soon as possible?

Not classical
A good teacher will also help you to discover the type of music which appeals to you most. Because clarinettists mainly play classical music, many clarinet teachers tend to give 'classical' lessons. But some teachers are equally at home in other musical styles, if not more so.

Looking for a teacher?
On page 132 you'll find details of several organizations which can tell you how to find teachers and music schools in your area. You can also search for private teachers in the small ads in newspapers, on notice boards in music shops and supermarkets, or in the *Yellow Pages*.

Listening and playing
And finally: listen to as much music as you can, both the kind of things you want to play and other music too. One of the best ways to learn is to watch other musicians at work, whether they're professional or amateur – so go to as many concerts as you can. And the very best way to learn how to play? Play a lot!

PRACTISING
What goes for every instrument is especially true for wind instruments: it's better to practise for half an hour every day than a whole day once a week. This is definitely the case with your embouchure: if you don't play for a few days, you'll feel it straight away.

Three times ten
If you find practising for half an hour a day hard going, try dividing it up into two quarter-hour sessions or three of ten minutes each.

In tune
Practice is also important for learning to play your instrument properly in tune. The longer you play and the more you learn to listen to yourself, the easier it will be.

Neighbours

Few instruments can be played as softly as the clarinet, but of course you won't always play softly. If neighbours or housemates are bothered by your playing, it may be enough simply to agree on fixed practice times. If you really play a lot, though, it may be better to insulate a room: even a very large cupboard can be big enough. There are plenty of books available on sound insulation, or you can hire a specialized contractor.

On CD

Playing the clarinet is something you usually do in a group, so it's often more fun to practise together too – even if there aren't any other musicians around. There are all kinds of CDs available to play along to, in all kinds of styles, and for beginners as well as for more advanced clarinettists. Your own part is omitted, leaving only the other musicians.

Computer lessons

If you have a computer handy, you can also use special CD-ROMs to practise with. Some have entire orchestral accompaniments on them; you can decide for yourself how fast you want a piece to be played and which parts you want to hear.

Metronome

Many pieces of music require you to keep to a constant speed, and practising with a metronome helps you achieve

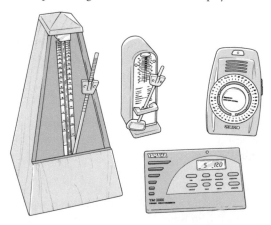

Two mechanical (clockwork) and two electronic metronomes

this. A metronome is a small clockwork or electronic device which ticks or bleeps out a steady adjustable pulse, so you can tell immediately if you start to play too fast or slow.

Recording

You can learn a lot by listening carefully to yourself playing, and that's why many musicians record themselves when they practise. If you record your clarinet lessons, you can listen to them again when you get home, paying attention to what was said and especially to how you sounded. All you need is a personal stereo with a built-in microphone. Better equipment (a separate microphone, for instance) is more expensive, but the recordings are usually more enjoyable to listen to.

4. BUYING A CLARINET

In this chapter you'll find out what you need to know before you go out to get yourself a clarinet – how much you can expect to spend, where you should go, and whether you should consider buying secondhand or renting an instrument. You'll find all the important technical details as well as tips for testing and comparing instruments in Chapter 5, A Good Clarinet.

The most inexpensive clarinets, costing around £300–400, are made of plastic. They usually come with a case and a mouthpiece, and often include one or two reeds as well. Plastic clarinets are unlikely to crack, they're nice and light and need relatively little maintenance.

Wood
From around £500–700 you can buy a wooden clarinet, which will give you a more beautiful, warmer tone. A slightly more expensive clarinet may well also have a better mechanism – which will last longer, need to be regulated less often and perform better.

Silver plated
If you spend a bit more money, you can get an instrument with a mechanism which is silver-plated instead of nickel-plated. This makes the clarinet look nicer, and it has the added advantage of making the keys feel 'stickier' to the touch, which means your fingers are less likely to slip off them.

Mid-range
Clarinettists who have been playing for a few years often

have instruments costing between £800 and £1000. This extra money usually buys you a clarinet which plays and sounds better: better materials will have been used and more care will have been devoted to its construction. It's not always easy to tell a higher-priced instrument from its appearance – mainly because even most cheaper instruments look very good.

Professional

Professional clarinettists and conservatory students often play instruments costing more than £1500. The more you spend, the harder it becomes to hear or see the differences.

The most expensive clarinets cost around £5000, or even more in some instances. At this price range, though, most clarinettists will buy a *pair* of clarinets – a B flat and an A. Obviously enough, this can double the price.

Other clarinets

Bass clarinets are a lot bigger and fewer of them are made, which means they cost a lot more. You can expect to pay £1200 for a plastic one, and the most expensive wooden bass clarinets can easily cost four times as much. E flat clarinets are smaller than B flat clarinets, but they're not generally any cheaper because the E flat is a specialist instrument not played by many people. You hardly find them in the lowest price range.

THE SHOP

A clarinet is a precision instrument which needs to be properly maintained and regulated. It also needs a full overhaul now and again. That's why you might be best off buying your instrument in a shop where they do these jobs themselves. This way you can be sure that they know what they're doing, and hopefully

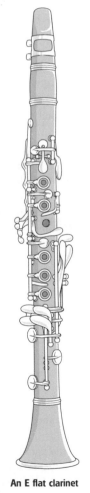

An E flat clarinet

they won't send you home with an instrument that plays badly. Even new clarinets need to be checked and regulated before they play well.

Overhaul

Every clarinet needs to be checked and readjusted from time to time. If you've bought a new instrument, that service may be free the first time it's needed or for the first year. Some shops and technicians will send you a reminder when it's time for an overhaul.

Another shop

When you're going to buy an instrument, it can't do any harm to visit a few different shops or clarinet workshops. Every shop sounds different when you're trying the instrument out, and you'll hear contrasting advice and opinions depending on where you go. What's more, not every shop will stock every brand.

Time and space

The more clarinets there are to choose from, the harder the choice can be – but looked at a different way, the better your chances are of finding exactly the clarinet you're looking for. Be sure to take your time, and remember that it's better to come back another time than to play for a few hours in a row. Some shops have a separate practice room so you don't bother the other customers – and the other way round.

On approval

In some cases you may be able to take an instrument on approval so that you can assess it at home at your leisure. This is more common with expensive clarinets than cheap ones, and you're more likely to be given the option if you already play than if you're choosing your first instrument. The major advantage of trying out a clarinet at home is that you know how your existing instrument sounds there, which helps you to compare properly. In a shop everything sounds different – even your own clarinet.

Not the same

Even two 'identical' clarinets will never sound exactly the same. So always buy the instrument you thought sounded best, not an 'identical' one from the warehouse. The same goes for mouthpieces.

Another clarinettist
In order to hear the differences between one clarinet and another, you need to be able to play well, which can be a problem if you're going to buy your first instrument. So take someone who can play with you, or go to a shop where a member of the sales staff plays the clarinet.

RENTING
You can also rent a clarinet at first. You can get yourself one for three months for as little as £40. Some shops rent them out per quarter; others only for longer periods. What exactly you'll pay varies. Sometimes it's 25 percent of the value of the instrument when new annually, in other cases it's 40 percent. That may depend on what the fee covers. Always check whether insurance and maintenance of the instrument are included in the rental charge, or whether you have to take care of these yourself. When renting, you'll always have to pay a deposit. Usually that will be between 10 and 25 percent of the value when new.

. . . and then buying
If you later want to buy the clarinet you've been renting, all or part of the rental fee you've paid so far may be deducted from the price. This may depend on the length of the agreed rental period. So always read your rental contract through properly before you sign it.

SECONDHAND
You can buy a properly checked and adjusted secondhand clarinet that you'll be able to play for years for as little as £150–200. Of course, you can also spend much more than that – some secondhand clarinets cost thousands. One of the advantages of a good secondhand instrument is that you'll probably be able to sell it again for a good price, provided it's been well-maintained.

At home or in a shop
Most secondhand clarinets are sold through music shops,

but they're also offered for sale in the small ads in newspapers, on notice boards in supermarkets and on the Internet. If you buy an instrument through an ad, you may pay less than in a shop. After all, the shop owner needs to make some money too.

In a music shop

All the same, buying from a music shop does have advantages. The instrument should have been checked and regulated, and you'll usually get a guarantee. And you can always go back if you have any questions, you can usually choose between a number of instruments, and in some cases you can even exchange the secondhand clarinet you bought for a different one within a certain period. Another advantage: a shop owner should never charge you much more than an instrument is worth. A private seller might, either because they don't know any better or because they think you don't.

A second opinion

If you're going to check out a secondhand instrument, it's even more important to take an experienced player along with you, especially if you're looking at a clarinet at someone's home. If you don't know what you're looking for or how to test for a good instrument, you might turn down a decent clarinet just because it's a bit dirty or get saddled with one that looks good but has a poor tone and is difficult to play in tune.

Valuation

If you really want to be sure you're not paying too much, get the instrument *appraised* (valued) first. A good shop or workshop can tell you exactly what a clarinet is worth, whether it needs any work done and what it will cost if so. You can find technical tips for secondhand instruments on page 59 and onwards.

Leaky

Any decent clarinet can be made to sound good, even if it leaks like a sieve and you can barely get a sound out of it. But if you buy an instrument like this, for instance through a newspaper ad, you should be aware that it might easily cost you £100 or more to get it fixed.

AND FINALLY

What you consider to be the best clarinet may well be the one your favourite clarinettist plays. Does that mean you should buy one like it? To be honest, there isn't much point. Even if you use exactly the same clarinet, the same mouthpiece and the same reed, you'll still sound different.

One on two, two on one

If you get a clarinettist to play two different clarinets you're not likely to hear much difference. But two different clarinettists on the same instrument won't sound the same at all. In other words, the sound depends more on the player than on the instrument.

The same

Even so, you'll sometimes see clarinettists in an orchestra playing the same brand of clarinet (they often have to), and even using the same type of mouthpiece. This is done to make the clarinettists sound as much as possible like a unified whole.

Brochures

If you want to know all about what's on sale, then go to a few shops and get hold of as many brochures as you can find, along with the relevant price lists.

Magazines, books and Internet

There are also various magazines you can buy if you want to read more about clarinets, and there are all kinds of books available, not to mention loads of stuff on the Internet. You'll find titles, addresses and other information on pages 131–132.

Clarinettists' gatherings

All kinds of get-togethers are organized for clarinettists, from clarinet conventions and courses to workshops and demonstrations. You can find out more about your instrument there – and you'll always learn something from the other clarinettists you meet. Check out some of the Websites listed on page 132 for more information.

5. A GOOD CLARINET

If you lay ten clarinets side by side, you'll barely see any difference between them. They're all the same shape, and all the keys, rings and holes are in the same places. Yet one may cost five times more than the next, one might sound much better and another might play more easily. This chapter explains why.

How a clarinet sounds depends more than anything else on you: a good clarinettist can make even the cheapest instrument sound impressive. Next in importance are the reed, the mouthpiece and the barrel. These three components are discussed separately in Chapters 6 and 7.

Many factors

There are many reasons why two clarinets might sound and play so differently. This chapter begins by looking at the materials that clarinets are made of. The next subject discussed is the inside of the clarinet (the *bore*), and then you can read about the toneholes (page 36), the mechanism (39), German clarinets (50) and secondhand instruments (59) – among other subjects.

With your ears

If you'd prefer to select a clarinet using your ears alone, then go straight to the tips for listening and play-testing on page 55 and onwards.

All the same

Clarinettists rarely agree about anything. The chapters which follow won't tell you who is right (often they all are), but rather what various experts think about different issues. You'll only discover who you agree with by playing and listening yourself – to clarinets and to clarinettists.

All clarinets

This book is mainly about the B flat clarinet, but most of what you read here also applies to all other clarinets. Here and there you'll find comments specifically about these other instruments.

MATERIALS

The cheapest clarinets are made of plastic, more expensive ones of wood, and in between are wooden instruments with a plastic bell and barrel. So what are the differences?

Plastic: the advantages

Plastic clarinets have many advantages. They are easier to make and therefore less expensive, they don't crack, they need less maintenance and they weigh about a quarter of a pound (around 100 grams) less than wooden instruments – especially good news for children.

Playing outdoors

Plastic clarinets are also very resistant to rain, freezing temperatures and sunshine, and you don't have to retune them as much when it gets colder or hotter.

Preferably wood

Despite the advantages of plastic, most clarinettists prefer to play wooden instruments. Wooden clarinets usually sound richer, darker and warmer, though this isn't all down to the material used – because they're more expensive, they are made more carefully and have a better quality mechanism.

Blacker and shinier

Plastic clarinets are usually easy to recognize, being blacker and shinier than wooden ones. However, some makers use plastics that look a little more like wood (*wood-grained polymers*), or make the surface of their plastic instruments a little less smooth. You may even come across clarinets in bright red, blue or other colours, especially in the US.

Attractive names

Because 'plastic' sounds so cheap, most manufacturers have come up with a more attractive name for it. Examples include Resotone, Resonite, Sonority Resin and Grena 2000.

Only the barrel and the bell

Some clarinets have only a barrel and a bell made of plastic. This helps to keep the price down, especially in the case of the bell: you need a fair-sized chunk of expensive wood to make a wooden bell. The sound of a clarinet like this will often noticeably improve if you replace the plastic barrel with a wooden one.

Wooden clarinets

Most wooden clarinets are made of an African wood variety which is extremely hard, heavy and very dark, indeed almost black in colour. It is usually called *grenadilla*, though you may come across other names in brochures such as African blackwood, M'pingo and ebony, or the technical name, dalbergia melanoxylon.

Other woods

Less common but sometimes also used for clarinets is West Indian ebony, which is also known as 'Brya Ebenus' or 'cocoswood'. Rosewood, a reddish-brown wood that is said to give a lighter, softer or sweeter tone, is even rarer.

Playing the clarinet in

In order to prevent a new wooden clarinet from cracking, it's best to play it in carefully. This way the wood, which has been dried in the factory, gets used to the moisture you blow into the instrument. One way to play your clarinet in would be to play it for quarter of an hour every day for the first week, and a quarter of an hour per day longer every following week. Or you could start with five minutes the first day, and add five more every day, or play half an hour a day for the first month, or . . .

Powder

The French brand Buffet (see page 118) also makes clarinets from a mixture of resin and compressed grenadilla powder, which they call *Green Line*. This material is considered virtually immune to cracks or splits and is

Larger clarinets, such as this bass clarinet which extends to low C, have metal necks, bows and bells

more resistant to dryness, moisture, cold and heat. At the same time, clarinets made from it are said to sound exactly or very much like wooden instruments.

Colour

Some brands give all their clarinets an extra-dark hue by staining them. Other brands don't colour them, and some brands give you the choice. There is no audible difference.

Metal parts

Large clarinets such as the alto and the bass have metal *necks* instead of barrels. The bell is just about always made of metal, too, as is the *bend* or *bow* which joins it to the instrument. Clarinet necks are often known as *crooks*.

Metal clarinets

In some folk music groups, including those from Turkey and Greece, you may see soprano clarinets made entirely of metal. You'd expect them to sound completely different, but in fact the contrast is not all that noticeable. Metal clarinets are a lot lighter, because the walls of the tube are very thin.

THE BORE

Many brochures give the width of the inside of the tube for each clarinet. This measurement, the bore, has a major effect on how an instrument sounds and plays.

A single-walled metal clarinet

Wide or narrow

Most clarinets have a bore of between 0.577" and 0.585" (14.65–14.85 mm), measured halfway up the instrument. The range may seem small on paper, but experienced players can tell the difference, finding that clarinets with wider bores blow slightly more easily, while those with a narrow *bore* have a little more resistance.

Wide

Clarinets with a really wide bore (up to 0.591"/15mm) are rarely used by beginners – they're not widely available and are harder to blow. Jazz clarinettists are likely to choose a bore like this: it requires more air, but you get more volume and a sound that can be described as big, hard, fat, thick or brash.

Narrow

For a lighter and more subdued 'classical' sound, you'll probably choose an instrument with a narrower bore.

Different country, different bore

Different countries have different styles of clarinet, mostly decided by the size of the bore. French clarinets usually have a narrow bore, Austrian and German instruments often have a fairly wide bore, whilst American models tend to be in between. In the UK there is something of a mixture between French and American styles, although wide-bored English clarinets have been regaining popularity in recent years.

Inches

Bore sizes are often given only in inches ("). To convert to millimetres, multiply that size by 25.4. For example, a 0.575" bore is 0.575 x 25.4 = 14.60mm.

Cylindrical

The tube of a clarinet is approximately the same width along the greater part of its length. To put it another way, a clarinet has a largely *cylindrical bore*. At certain points, though, the bore becomes narrower, or wider – such as at the bell.

Air column

The exact shape of the bore greatly affects the way in which a clarinet plays and sounds. Why is this? When you blow, the reed makes the air in the clarinet vibrate, and vibrating air is sound. In other words, this vibrating air column 'makes' the sound of the clarinet. The character of a clarinet's sound depends to a very large extent on the shape of the air column – and that shape is of course the same as the shape of the bore.

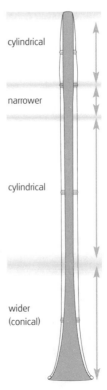

Conical

Towards its lower end, a clarinet becomes steadily wider. This part of the instrument has a *conical bore*. The conical section usually begins somewhere about halfway down the lower joint, and is of course most pronounced at the bell.

Reverse cone

At the top of the upper joint, the tube usually narrows by a near-invisible amount (*reverse cone*). This produces more resistance, and makes the sound darker, warmer, deeper and more

The shape of the air column is important for the character of the sound

colourful. A clarinet with an upper joint which doesn't get narrower towards the top, or which does so only by a very small amount, blows very easily and often has a rather bright, open sound – just like an instrument with a wide bore.

All kinds of names

Because this narrowing at the top is so important, all kinds

33

of words are used in brochures and books to describe that small section of the bore. For instance, a *linear cone* means that the tube becomes wider or narrower evenly, and *dual taper* means it does so in two steps (first a little more quickly then more gradually, or the other way around). Many instruments have a *polycylindrical* or a *polyconical bore*: a bore which narrows in three or more steps.

More, better, richer

All of this jargon is only really important to clarinet makers and not to players. After all, you don't buy a clarinet because it has a particular bore, but because of the way it plays and sounds. Of course, brochures do tell you lots of stuff about the supposed advantages of certain bores – increased volume, richer sound or a tone which is easier to control.

Smooth

If you look through the lower joint and upper joint of a clarinet, you can see how smoothly the bore is finished. A smooth bore allows an instrument to sound more easily and more evenly. If a secondhand clarinet has a messy-looking bore, that may be because it hasn't been kept clean properly – and it's therefore worth avoiding.

Wall thickness

Some clarinets have thicker walls than others. A thicker wall is said to give a 'thicker', more robust sound which carries further (it *projects* more). An instrument with thin walls usually responds better and sounds lighter, sweeter and less penetrating.

Big clarinets

Naturally enough, bigger clarinets have bigger bores. To give you an idea: the alto clarinet usually has a bore of between 0.670" and 0.710" (17–18mm), bass clarinets between 0.905" and 0.945" (23–24mm) and, at the other end of the scale, E flat clarinets are usually somewhere around 0.530" (13.5mm).

THE BELL

The bell is more important to the sound than you might think. It doesn't just influence the sound of the *long-tube notes*, which you play with all or almost all of the keys closed, but also the notes that sound from the middle section of the clarinet. Without the bell, your instrument sounds less resonant than it does with the bell attached.

Try it out

It follows that a clarinet will sound slightly different with one bell than with another. A bell which flares more widely can make the sound a little more open, for instance, and a bell with slightly thicker walls can make the sound a bit thicker. To be able to hear these differences you need to be a competent musician and have a good instrument – and if so, it can really be worthwhile experimenting with different bells.

Position

Some clarinettists with unusually sharp ears even carefully rotate the bell until they've found the position which allows the instrument to sound its very best. Once that position is decided, they always fit the bell in exactly that way.

For sale separately

Bells are sold separately not only to clarinettists looking for a better sound, but also to those who need to replace a broken bell. You can buy a new one from around £30. As ever, you can also pay a lot more: there are wooden bells for bass clarinets that cost thousands of pounds.

Bell ring

Because thin wooden bells are especially vulnerable, they usually have metal bell rings. Plastic clarinets have *bell rings* only for show, so some brands give you the choice between an instrument with a ring or without. Rings can come loose (on wooden instruments especially) and cause buzzes, and a ring makes the instrument heavier – though only by a very small amount.

No scratch protection

The bell ring almost never extends so far as to completely protect the wooden edge of the bell. That means that if you set down your clarinet on the bell, it won't be protected against scratches, so try to use a clarinet stand (see page

97). If you don't have one, it's obviously much better to lay the instrument down instead with its keys pointing upwards.

BODY RINGS AND TENON RINGS

Most clarinets have metal *body rings* wherever two joints meet. These rings, also known as *joint rings*, are said to make the sound a tiny bit darker. This is why some clarinets have only very thin body rings or none at all. The difference is easier to see than to hear, though.

Tenon rings

The cork-covered ends of the upper and lower joints are called the *tenons*. They are often reinforced with metal tips called *tenon rings*. On cheaper clarinets, not every tenon has a tenon ring.

A tenon without a tenon ring, and one with

Too-thick tenons

Once you've applied a little cork grease, always check how easily the barrel, lower joint, upper joint and bell fit together and come apart. If they slide apart too easily, there's a chance that air will leak. If they're too stiff, one of the tenons may need to have some cork removed, though the joints of a new clarinet always feel a bit stiff to begin with.

TONEHOLES

Clarinets have three kinds of toneholes: those with rings, those with keys and those with nothing at all. The toneholes with keys are recessed (*countersunk*) and have slightly bevelled edges to make sure that the pads stop the holes properly.

Rings

The toneholes with rings have a small *chimney* or *riser*, around which the ring falls. Some clarinets come with chimneys made from a different material than that of the instrument, often plastic or ebonite (hard rubber). These are said to give

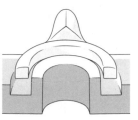

The ring falls around the chimney

a brighter sound and be less likely to crack or deform. Other instruments have *integral toneholes*, which means the toneholes are made from the same piece of wood as the tube (see page 116).

Raised tonehole

The tonehole under the left fourth finger is usually just a hole, without either a ring or a key. Every so often, though, a clarinet has a chimney for that tonehole, bringing the edge of the hole up to the same level as the rings so that all of your fingers go down the same distance.

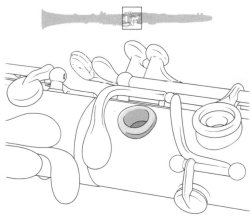

A raised D/A tonehole

Register tube

If you look through the upper joint of a clarinet, you'll see two small metal tubes or sleeves: the *register* or *speaker tube* inside the register key's tonehole, and another tube inside the thumbhole. These tubes stop the moisture you blow into your clarinet from running out through those holes. They also affect the sound of an instrument and its *intonation* – how naturally in tune it is. That's why German clarinets have register tubes, too, even though that particular tonehole is at the top of the tube so it can't get waterlogged.

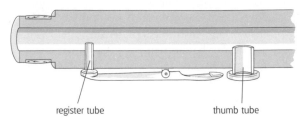

register tube   thumb tube

The long, narrow register tube and the slightly shorter, fatter thumb tube aren't just there to stop moisture running out

Undercut

Virtually all clarinets of a certain quality have *undercut toneholes*, which means every tonehole gets slightly wider on the inside. Undercut toneholes give an instrument a

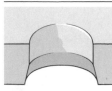

An undercut tonehole

darker tone, a quicker response and better intonation as well as generally making it sound more beautiful. If your instrument has straight toneholes – you only really find them on cheap clarinets – it's harder to correct your notes.

Extra holes

Some clarinets have extra holes to make particular notes sound better or more in tune. These *resonance holes* or *vent holes* may be open, or they may have keys.

Tuning

Most orchestras, ensembles and other groups tune to the *sounding* or *concert pitch* A – an A at normal pitch, not as it's played on a transposing instrument like the B flat clarinet. This is the A note slightly to the right of the centre of a piano keyboard (see page 9). If you play this key, the strings vibrate 440 times per second. In technical terms, the A equals 440 hertz.

Or a little higher

In some countries, orchestras, choirs and other groups

tend to tune a fraction higher than A=440 hertz, for instance to A=442. This ever-so-slightly higher tuning makes an orchestra sound just a little brighter or more brilliant. If you want to be properly in tune, your clarinet must be built to the tuning of the orchestra you're playing in. For this reason, some clarinets come in both 440 and 442 hertz versions. The toneholes are distributed along the clarinet slightly differently for each pitch. If you do occasionally need to make your instrument sound higher or lower, you can adjust your barrel or use one of a different size (see page 72).

THE MECHANISM

A clarinet mechanism must feel nice and smooth under your fingers, and should not rattle or produce other unwanted noises. A play-testing tip: if you 'play' without actually blowing, it's easy to tell whether the mechanism is quiet enough. Use all the keys, and pay special attention to the keys you work with your left little finger – because they're the longest they can often cause the most noise if things aren't quite right.

A proper seal

The mechanism must ensure that all the keys close tightly. If a key doesn't shut perfectly, you won't be able to play that note – and possibly lots of others – properly, if at all. Usually it's a matter of adjustment, but a torn pad can also cause a key to leak (see page 49).

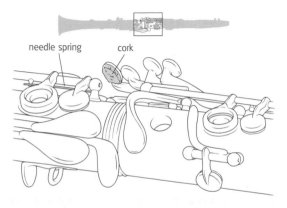

needle spring   cork

The springs must be adjusted to make all the keys feel the same

An even feel

Each key has a spring which makes sure the key opens again after you've closed it or the other way around. Some keys use *needle springs*, which do indeed look like needles. The trill keys, the A key and the register key (sometimes called the *see-saw keys*) have *leaf springs*: narrow, springy metal strips. The springs should be adjusted in such a way that all the keys feel even.

Too stiff or too light

Keys that are too stiff make playing difficult, but if your keys move too easily, you may find that you can't feel what you're doing properly or that the keys become sluggish and don't return to their positions as quickly as they should. If a spring is adjusted much too lightly there's even a risk that you'll blow the key open when you play loudly.

Rings

If the rings are adjusted so that they are too high when they open, it's hard to stop the toneholes. And if they're too low, the coupled keys won't respond immediately as they should. Some clarinettists prefer their rings to have a fairly high adjustment; others prefer rings that are on the low side.

Fit properly

Some clarinets seem to suit large hands, small hands, fat fingers or thin ones. You probably won't notice such differences fully until you take the time to play an instru-

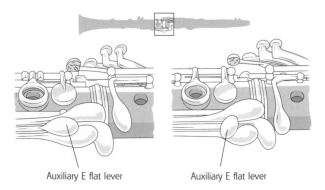

Auxiliary E flat lever   Auxiliary E flat lever

The differences are often greatest by the left little finger levers. Look at the (auxiliary) E flat lever in particular

ment. The position and shape of the left little finger levers in particular can vary. Some brands have cheap clarinets with mechanisms made especially for very small hands – so even quite young children should be able to find one to fit.

Adjustable thumbrest

An adjustable thumbrest may make the instrument more comfortable to play. Some clarinets have an adjustment bolt that you can undo and tighten with a coin – handy if you don't have a screwdriver on you. If your instrument has a fixed thumbrest, you can easily have it replaced with an adjustable one. If the thumbrest cuts into your thumb, you can buy a rubber *thumb saver*, which fits over it, for a pound or two.

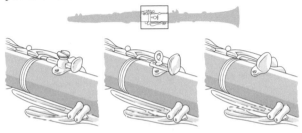

A thumbrest which you can adjust with a coin, an adjustable one with a ring and a simple, fixed thumbrest

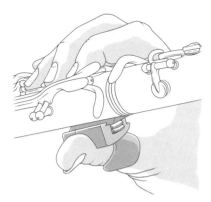

Adjustable thumbrest (Ton Kooiman Etude)

Special thumbrests

When you play the entire weight of the clarinet (a good pound or two) rests on the furthest joint of your thumb.

This can cause pain or discomfort, especially when you're playing for long stretches at a time. To avoid this, there are special thumbrests which divert the weight of the clarinet onto the first joint. You can have this type of thumbrest made to order, but you can also buy them off the shelf. One specialized company which supplies them is Ton Kooiman.

Neck strap
Another way to reduce the pressure on the thumb is to use a neck strap (see page 16). Although typically used by children, these are increasingly popular with adult clarinettists.

Nickel-plated or silver-plated
On clarinets costing up to around £400 the keywork is usually nickel-plated, while on more expensive instruments it is almost always silver-plated. Sometimes you can choose – if so, the silver plated mechanism might cost around £30–50 extra.

The differences
The difference between keys that are nickel-plated and ones that are silver-plated is clearly visible: nickel has a slightly 'harder' shine than silver. Nickel is cheaper, it needs less polishing and is more resilient than silver. But nickel feels more slippery, which can be a problem if you perspire when you play, so many players are willing to play the extra. What's more, some people suffer from an allergy to nickel.

Gold
If you have very acid perspiration, it can make silver tarnish so quickly that you're better off with a nickel-plated mechanism. Or you could even have your keywork gold-plated instead. New clarinets with fully or partly gold-plated mechanism are rare, though sometimes only the *posts* are gold-plated.

Posts
The posts are the small pillars which fasten the mechanism to the clarinet. In many cases, some of the posts will have an extra screw to stop them from twisting out of position under the pressure of the needle springs.

Some of the posts are anchored

Rounded or pointed keys

Almost all clarinets have so-called *French-style keys*: that means they are attached to the key rod by an arm which ends in a point. The pad cups or key cups which actually stop the toneholes come in two varieties: *rounded* (also called *rond-bombé*) or slightly pointed (*conical* or *China cup*). Virtually all clarinets have *power-forged* keys, meaning that they are shaped by pressure, when the metal is cold, rather than cast.

Trill keys

The trill keys, too, come in two types. On some clarinets there is a kink in the long shafts of the keys just before the pad cups (*offset trill keys*); on others these shafts are straight (*inline trill keys*). The movement of the pad cup is a little more logical with the inline system – it moves vertically up and down, rather than slightly diagonally.

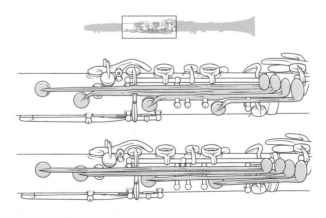

Inline and offset trill keys

Not that it makes much difference: you find both systems on cheap and expensive instruments alike.

Separate rods

What does make a difference is whether certain keys are mounted on their 'own', separate key rods. If so, they tend to be easier to regulate, and the mechanism lasts longer. On most more expensive clarinets, each trill key has its own key rod, while on cheaper instruments the B flat and B keys share one rod. Some budget clarinets also have only three posts underneath the A and A flat keys instead of four. More expensive clarinets may have extra key rods – for instance on the C sharp/G sharp and the A flat/E flat keys.

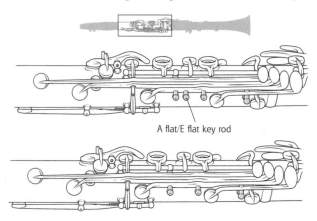

A flat/E flat key rod

The adjustment screws for the F sharp/C sharp and the E/B keys are in the crow foot, by the right little finger

Adjustment screws

Pretty much all clarinets have an adjustment screw on the A and A flat/G sharp keys, on the upper part of the left-hand joint. In order to make those two coupled keys move together smoothly, this screw needs to be properly adjusted. You'll find other adjustment screws only on more expensive clarinets – typically the F sharp/C sharp and E/B keys will be adjustable, with two extra screws under the *crow foot* by your right little finger. Very occasionally, the F/C key will also have an adjustment screw, or the bridge will. Of course, a clarinet can also be adjusted without screws, but only with some very careful bending. A job for a professional, in other words.

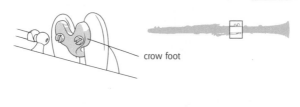

crow foot

The adjustment screws for the F sharp/C sharp and the E/B keys are in the crow foot, by the right little finger

Cork
Some keys need to be adjusted by sticking pieces of cork of varying thickness under them – a job which in most cases is better left to a specialist. Those corks also make the mechanism quieter: they prevent the metal pad cups from touching metal or wood.

Large clarinets and German clarinets
Larger clarinets, which have much longer key rods, usually have even more adjustment screws – and clarinets with German mechanisms often have a lot too.

EXTRA KEYS
The great majority of Boehm clarinets have a regular mechanism with seventeen keys and six rings (*17/6 clarinets*), but there are a few which have some extra keys and other options.

Auxiliary E flat lever
Sometimes you'll notice four levers by the left little finger instead of the usual three. That extra fourth lever, the *auxiliary E flat lever*, is for the A flat/E flat key, which you can normally only operate with your right little finger. Some more expensive clarinets have this auxiliary lever (also known as *auxiliary E flat/A flat*) as standard. If you don't use it, you can remove it or have it removed. Other models come either with or without the extra lever – if you choose to have it, you'll pay more.

Fork B flat
With the addition of a seventh ring key by your right index finger, you can play a B flat by pressing down your

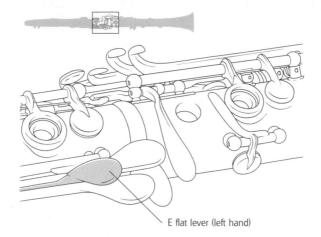

E flat lever (left hand)

The auxiliary E flat lever: the fourth lever by your left little finger

left ring finger and index finger at the same time: this *forked fingering* is called a *fork B flat*. That seventh ring also makes certain trills easier.

Articulated G sharp

Much rarer than the fork B flat is the *articulated G sharp* or *F sharp/G sharp trill key*. You can identify an articulated G sharp by the extra closed hole key under the G sharp lever and the extra lever on the lower joint. This system enables you to play all kinds of trills on G sharp or C sharp with your right index finger instead of your left little finger, making trilling easier.

Low E flat

A clarinet with a low E flat is just a little longer; you play this extra low note with a fifth key by your right little finger.

Why are these not standard?

A clarinet with all of these extras is called a *full-Boehm* instrument. Only a few manufacturers still make them. How come? For several reasons: all the additions make the instrument a lot heavier and the tone less bright; the articulated G sharp is complicated mechanically; and the seventh ring makes some trills easier but others impossible. Which is why almost everyone uses a 17/6 instrument instead: it's the best compromise.

Low E vent key

Other additions are available too. For example, some French clarinets have a so-called *low E vent key*. If you play a low E or F, a key opens above an extra tonehole at the end of the lower joint or in the bell. This slightly raises those two notes, which often sound a little flat, especially on German clarinets – and as a result, low E vent keys are much more common on those instruments.

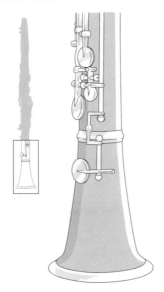

An extra key for the low E and F on a German clarinet

Improved B flat

Because of the complicated acoustics of the clarinet there is hardly a clarinet in existence which can produce a throat B flat (the B flat above middle C) that sounds really good, unless you play it using a different fingering such as with the side trill key. If you don't, you use

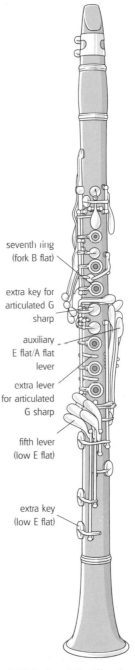

seventh ring
(fork B flat)

extra key for
articulated G
sharp

auxiliary
E flat/A flat
lever

extra lever
for articulated
G sharp

fifth lever
(low E flat)

extra key
(low E flat)

A full-Boehm clarinet (Amati)

47

the same tonehole for this B flat as for the register key. In order to make that note sound really good, the tonehole would actually need to be a bit bigger and a bit lower – but then it would be too big and too low to serve as the tonehole for the register key.

Extra key

This is why clarinets using the German system often have an extra key to make the sound of the throat B flat a little clearer. Many solutions have been provided to improve its pitch, such as an adjustable attachment designed to sit on top of the A tonehole – which can be bought separately and whose size can be adjusted to produce the desired pitch.

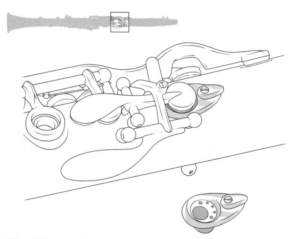

Adjustable tonehole to improve the throat B flat (Tutz)

Bass clarinet to low C

Bass clarinets always have a low E flat, and many go down to a low C. How you play those lowest notes depends on the brand, and sometimes even on the model. You might have to operate three keys with your right thumb and five with your little finger, or two with your thumb and six with your little finger. A bass clarinet which goes down to low C can easily cost £1000 more than the same instrument with E flat as its lowest note.

Second register key

In order to improve response and allow you to play better in tune, some alto and bass clarinets have two register keys. Which of the two keys you open depends on the note you are playing. For some notes in the highest register, bass clarinets also have a small extra hole in the pad cup under your left index finger: to play the notes in question you close the key but leave the hole open.

PADS

To ensure that the pad cups seal the toneholes properly they are fitted with pads on the inside. Usually a pad consists of a layer of felt covered with a very thin membrane, which is often called *fish skin* but which is actually made from cow intestine. Because this material tears very easily, two or even three layers are often used.

Plastic

Plastic pads, which generally cost a little more, are becoming more and more common on clarinets. They are not affected by moisture or dryness as much as traditional pads, and they last longer too. One well-known brand name is Gore-Tex.

Leather

German clarinets and some other instruments often have pads made of very thin goat leather, which supposedly make the tone a little darker than skin pads. Leather pads, too, are increasingly being replaced by plastic.

Cork

The keys at the bottom of the tube may have cork pads, because they are the most likely to become waterlogged by the moisture that collects in the instrument. Bass clarinets and other clarinets may have cork pads on other keys, too.

Resonators

Some clarinets have metal *resonators* in the pads of the last keys of the lower joint, adding a little to their brightness and projection.

THE A CLARINET

Clarinettists in a symphony orchestra almost always have two clarinets: a B flat clarinet and a slightly longer A

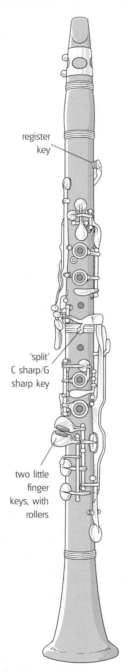

register
key

'split'
C sharp/G
sharp key

two little
finger
keys, with
rollers

**A German clarinet with
the Albert system**

clarinet, which goes a semitone lower. Though some composers have written specifically for the A clarinet's slightly darker sound, the main reason for using it is because in certain keys it's a lot easier to play. A part in concert-pitch A major, for instance, means five sharps for a B flat clarinet but none at all for an A clarinet: if you're playing the latter instrument, you simply play in C major.

Different?

The A clarinet is said to sound a little darker, mellower and richer than a B flat clarinet. Some clarinettists think the difference is quite marked, others say you only really hear it well at the bottom end of the highest register.

GERMAN CLARINETS

In Germany and Austria most clarinettists play German clarinets. These have a slightly different sound, and also a different mechanism. This mechanism comes in many different variations. *Albert*, *Oehler* and *reform-Boehm* are the three best known systems.

Sound

German clarinets sound different to French ones. But opinions are divided as to exactly how different. Some say the difference is small, but many think that German clarinets sound darker, more robust, thicker, fuller or sweeter, with the French (Boehm) sound being described as brighter, lighter, more open and delicate.

Different bore

The contrast in sound between German and French clarinets lies largely in the bore. One difference is that German clarinets only begin to flare out beyond the E/B key, rather than halfway down the lower joint. In other words, the cylindrical section of the bore is much longer than on a French instrument. The mouthpiece and reed are different, too – as you can read in the chapters that follow.

Wider or narrower?

When it comes to the difference in bore sizes, the picture is confused – some people say that the bore of German clarinets is wider than that of French instruments, but others claim precisely the opposite. The truth is that both are right: bores vary from brand to brand. While one German clarinet maker uses a narrow bore of around 0.575" (14.6mm), which is slightly narrower than most French ones, another goes for a wide bore of 0.590" (15mm), which is as wide as the widest French bore.

Little fingers keys

The easiest way to tell you're looking at a German clarinet is by the right-hand little-finger keys. There are only two of them, with a roller to help you move from key to key. The left little finger keys are different, too.

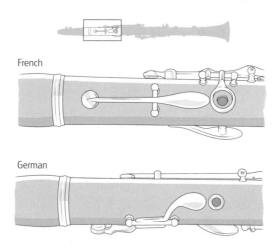

French

German

On German clarinets, the register key lever is nearer the front of the tube

Split and bowed

If you look carefully you'll notice other differences, too: for instance, the C sharp/G sharp key is 'split' so that you can also operate it with your right little finger. The lever of the register key also has a large bow in it because the hole it covers is near the front of the tube, not the back.

Albert system

German clarinets come with various different mechanisms. In Germany and Austria, students usually start out on an instrument with the *Albert system*, which has nineteen or twenty keys and between four and six ring keys. These clarinets are rarely used in other countries, though you may find them being played in concert bands and other wind bands or in Dixieland groups. Often they will be older instruments.

Oehler system

Most advanced and professional German clarinettists play instruments with the *Oehler system*. You can recognize an Oehler clarinet by the one plateau key by the right middle finger and by the two F-resonance keys on the lower joint. Those two extra keys make the F and the low B flat brighter and better in tune.

Full-Oehler

Oehler clarinets come in all kinds of variations. The simplest version has twenty-one keys, and so-called *full-Oehlers* may have as many as twenty-seven.

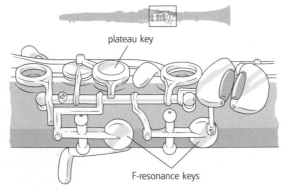

plateau key

F-resonance keys

The Oehler system is easy to recognize by the plateau key (Griffdeckel) near the right middle finger and the two F-resonance keys on the side

Why French?

One reason why the French system is favoured in most countries around the world is because it's easier to play than the German one. You need fewer fork fingerings (see pages 45–46), and certain notes can be played in a wider variety of ways.

German with French

The reform-Boehm or German Boehm clarinet allows you to play with a French mechanism but produce a German sound. This type of clarinet has a German bore, and hence a German sound, but a French Boehm mechanism. However, the mechanism may differ slightly from a standard Boehm instrument – it may have a double F/C key, for example, or rollers between the right little finger keys. German Boehm clarinets are often used by members of Dutch symphony orchestras, but are quite rare outside mainland Europe.

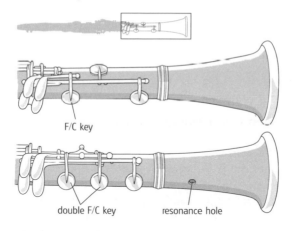

F/C key

double F/C key   resonance hole

A regular Boehm clarinet with a single F/C key, and a German Boehm with a double F/C key and a resonance hole

Even more systems

There are many other lesser-known systems as well, such as the Schmidt-Kolbe system (which features lots of additional keys), and the old Müller system. Clarinets like these are hardly found outside central Europe. One notable exception is Austria, where clarinet players use *Austrian clarinets*, with a wide bore and a mechanism that varies slightly from the Oehler system.

Deutsche System

The Albert system is known in Germany as the *Deutsche system* (German system). The name Albert is only really used outside Germany.

IN TUNE

In order to play really well in tune, you need to correct certain notes – even on the best clarinets, though the better an instrument, the more inherently in tune it will be and the less correcting you need to do. In technical terms, the better a clarinet's *intonation*, the less you have to do to play in tune.

Out of tune

In order to be able to judge a clarinet's intonation you need to be able to play pretty well. Otherwise you'll never know whether it's the clarinet that is out of tune or whether it's just you.

Too small, too big

A clarinet could be made to play more in tune if it had three or more register keys, but that would make the mechanism much too complicated. So there is only one, and that one register key can never be in the ideal position for every tone combination (E/B, F/C and so on).

Always different

But it's not just the register key which determines the intonation of a clarinet – other contributory factors include the position and shape of the toneholes, the bore, the barrel and the mouthpiece. Every manufacturer has its own solutions to make the intonation of its clarinets as good as possible, so which notes you have to correct and by how much can vary from one brand to another, and even from one model to another.

All the same

Because the tuning can vary from one clarinet to the next, some groups and orchestras prefer all their clarinettists to play the same type of instrument. This won't mean the tuning will always be perfect, but it will mean the clarinet section is more likely to sound like a unified whole.

All different

Every clarinet is different. So when you buy a new instrument, you first need to discover which notes you need to correct by how much. Take this into account when you're play-testing clarinets. But be careful: if you're used to a clarinet on which a certain note tends to sound much too low (or *flat*), that note may suddenly seem much too high (or *sharp*) on a 'better' clarinet because you are compensating too much for it. That can make a better clarinet sound more out of tune than it really is.

Only a few

Though there are a few notes that are either too sharp or flat on most clarinets, every instrument has its own problem notes. The notes which vary most between instruments are generally those you play with most of the keys open, g' to b♭' (see page 14). These are called the *short-pipe* or *short-tube notes*, because you only use a 'short' section of the clarinet to make them.

Too short, too low . . .

Sometimes certain notes may be too high or too low by such an amount that you can never get them properly in tune. This may be caused by having the wrong mouthpiece or barrel on the instrument, or because certain keys are opening too far (or not far enough). A key that doesn't open far enough produces a note which is too low, and it will also sound slightly stuffy. If the *key opening* or *venting* is too big, the note will be too high.

TIPS FOR TESTING

A good clarinet not only sounds as in tune as possible, it also has a beautiful tone – and what counts as a beautiful tone depends mainly on your taste and the type of music you play. And that's not all: a good clarinet will also sound even, whether you play loudly or softly, high or low and long-tube or short-tube notes.

Another player

In order to choose a clarinet by its sound, you need to be able to play reasonably well. If you can't play or haven't been playing very long, take a good clarinettist with you to try out the following listening and play-testing tips, or go to a shop with a clarinettist on staff.

Somebody else

If you get someone else to play a number of clarinets for you, they'll never sound the same as if you were to play them yourself – but you will be able to hear the differences between the various instruments. A tip: even if you do play yourself, ask somebody else to play for you just to hear how various clarinets sound from a distance. You'll find you hear things you didn't hear before. If there's no other clarinettist you can ask, point the instrument at a wall so that the sound is reflected back towards you.

The barrel and mouthpiece

Only if you play every clarinet with the same mouthpiece and barrel will you hear the differences between the instruments – rather than the differences between the mouthpieces and barrels. Preferably use your own mouthpiece and barrel to start with, but do be aware that some clarinets will perform better with a different combination.

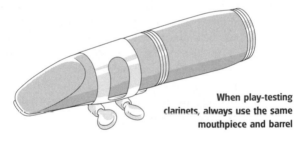

When play-testing clarinets, always use the same mouthpiece and barrel

Briefly at first

If you have a whole selection of clarinets in front of you, choosing is often easiest if you only play each instrument briefly. Play something simple, otherwise you'll be concentrating more on playing than on listening – scales, for instance, and make them nice and slow.

Sheet music

If you are used to playing from sheet music, take a few pieces with you when you go to choose a clarinet. The better you know a piece, the less you'll be thinking about the notes and the closer you can listen.

Two by two

Once you've found a number of clarinets that you really like, compare them two by two or three by three. Choose the best one and replace the one you like least with another clarinet. Again choose the best one, and so on. In order to choose the very best clarinet from the two or three that remain, you may want to play each instrument a little longer so that you get to know it better. But even after just fifteen minutes' playing it gets harder to hear the differences between clarinets. Take a break, or come back a day or two later.

With your ears alone

Try listening to the same clarinets without looking to see which one you're playing. This way you're making a choice with your ears alone, without being influenced by the price, the brand name or anything else. If the clarinet which sounds best and plays best turns out to be the cheapest one too, that's a bonus.

No idea

If you have no idea where to start when you walk into a shop, ask for two clarinets with very different sounds – one with a notably dark tone and another which sounds particularly bright, for example. Decide which one you like and go on from there. Or try a very cheap clarinet alongside the most expensive one in the shop, simply to hear how much difference it makes.

Your own clarinet

Take your own clarinet with you to the shop, if you have one. This makes it easier to hear just how different the other instruments sound. But be aware that you may be so used to your own instrument that it may seem to sound better or better in tune than other clarinets – even much more expensive ones.

WHAT TO LISTEN FOR

Comparing the sounds of different clarinets is something you have to learn how to do; the more often you do it, the more you'll hear. But first of all you need to know what kind of things to listen out for. Read on . . .

What you like

When two people listen to the same clarinet, they often use completely different words to describe what they hear. What one person considers shrill and thin (and therefore not attractive), another may consider bright, brilliant and clear (and therefore good). And what one player describes as dark, round and velvety, another may think dull and blunt. It all depends on what you like – and the words you use to describe it.

Character

What sounds good and what doesn't also depends on the kind of music you play. If you play classical music, you're probably looking for a darker, warmer sound than if you play jazz or folk. But of course there are clarinets which allow you to play different styles fairly easily – they have a sound that is very versatile and easy to correct.

Easy

Some clarinets blow more easily than others, and this is mainly down to the bore. It's often said that a clarinet with a wide bore blows more easily and has a bigger, more open tone – though it's not easy to tell the difference if you haven't been playing for long. Classical players usually prefer an instrument with more resistance and a darker sound, though if a clarinet has too much resistance the sound becomes dull and lifeless.

Resistance

When you play long-tube notes you'll always feel more resistance or pressure than when you play short-tube ones. That difference is bigger with some clarinets than others. The smaller the difference, the easier it is to make the instrument sound even – whether you're playing high, low, short-tube or long-tube notes.

High and low

The high notes sound different from the low ones on all clarinets, but the better the instrument, the smaller the difference will be. The low notes should sound firm, deep and clear even when you're playing softly, and the high notes must not sound shrill, strident or metallic even when you're playing loud.

Loud and soft

To see how a clarinet performs, go from high to low playing loudly and then do the same playing softly. Notice whether the instrument responds equally easily whether you make each note sound separately (*staccato*), or join all the notes together (*legato*).

Rising and falling

When you go from loud to soft, and the other way around, check that the notes don't become higher or lower to any great degree. On clarinets, the pitch has a tendency to fall as you get louder and to rise when you play more softly – this is unusual, as with most other instruments it's the other way around.

Problem notes

When you are comparing the sounds of different clarinets, pay special attention to the notes from g' to b♭' (see page 14). These are the clarinet's 'problem notes' – those which clarinet makers find hardest to get sounding good. The B flat is particularly tricky. If that note sounds really good, you're likely to have an excellent clarinet in your hands.

Break

The group of tricky short-tube notes between the chalumeau register and the clarinet register is sometimes called the *throat register* or the *break register*.

SECONDHAND

When you go to buy a secondhand clarinet, there are a few extra things you should remember. To begin with, always put the clarinet together yourself, so you can check that the fit between components is good. They should fit together so snugly that the clarinet feels as though it was made from a single piece of wood.

Leaky

Check that all the notes respond well. If not, there's a fair chance that air is leaking somewhere. That could be down to a torn pad, a poorly adjusted ring or key or a leak between two joints. Air can also escape from around the register tube. A play-testing tip: take off the upper joint, close all the toneholes and block one end with your hand, put your lips around the other end and suck. If you inhale any air, there is a leak somewhere. Then do the same with the lower joint – you can blow instead if you want to. When you blow hard, you might find that the C sharp and E flat keys on the lower joint open of their own accord. If this happens, their springs should be adjusted to provide a little more resistance.

Play

Check carefully that keys and levers can only move up and down, not backwards and forwards. Older instruments often suffer from play on the F sharp/C sharp and the E/B by the left little finger. This makes playing uncomfortable and causes leaks and unwanted noises. What's more, it can only get worse.

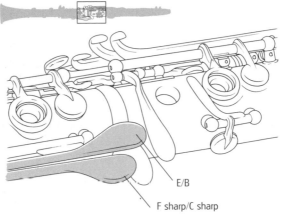

E/B

F sharp/C sharp

Play is especially common here

Buzzes

Other unwanted noises may be due to poor regulation, a missing cork, torn pads, loose or missing springs or a loose metal bell ring, tenon ring or body ring. If a ring is loose, it may be that the clarinet has been stored in conditions which have been too dry for too long, which increases the chance that the wood will crack at some point in the future.

Cracks

Wooden clarinets always need to be checked for cracks. The most likely places to find them are on the tenons of all the components and the toneholes by the A and A flat/G sharp keys and the trill keys. Cracks aren't necessarily the end, though: small ones can often be repaired effectively.

Dirt
Look down through the bore, not forgetting the barrel and the mouthpiece. If the previous owner took good care of the instrument, everything will look smooth on the inside and it will smell of clarinet and not dank or musty.

Mouthpiece
Also inspect the outside of the mouthpiece. If there are teeth marks, your own teeth will be forced into the same position. Check the edges, too: even minor damage can make a mouthpiece unusable. In the following chapter you will read why even a good mouthpiece may be no use to you.

Valuation
It's always a good idea to have a used clarinet *appraised* (valued) by an expert. Then you'll know what it's worth and what it might cost you to have it regulated or repaired. To give you some idea, a crack can often be repaired for around £25, a set of new tenons might cost three times as much, and for about £100–150 you can get an old, worn-out clarinet made as good as new.

6. MOUTHPIECES, LIGATURES AND BARRELS

Although the way in which clarinets sound depends chiefly on who is playing them, almost as important are reeds (which are covered in Chapter 7), mouthpieces and barrels. Even the ligature of an instrument affects the sound.

Some mouthpieces play more easily than others. If you're just starting out, it's nice to have a mouthpiece that plays easily – but you won't get a really beautiful, dark tone out of it. If you've been playing a little longer, the best mouthpiece is one which allows you to play loudly or softly, high or low and staccato or legato with equal ease.

Right for the clarinet

You can't simply put any mouthpiece on any clarinet. A poorly chosen mouthpiece can make the instrument sound out of tune, too strident, too dull or very uneven.

Right for the player

A mouthpiece also has to suit you. That includes your embouchure, your technique and the sound you're looking for. One person may play beautifully with a mouthpiece that someone else can't even get a decent note out of.

Almost anyone

Some mouthpieces are designed to be as versatile as possible, while not at a huge cost. These usually cost somewhere between £30 and £60, and make good replacements for the cheap mouthpieces that come with budget clarinets. A clarinet fitted with a cheap mouthpiece will often sound too shrill and harsh. What's more, cheap mouthpieces often don't play very easily, which can make half an hour's practice seem like a very long time.

Keep looking

Once you've found a better mouthpiece, it will give you a good point of reference if you later decide to try out some more different ones. And there are more than enough to choose from, from budget models right up to handmade mouthpieces costing more than £200.

In brief

When you go out to buy a mouthpiece, you'll almost certainly come across certain technical terms:

- The *tip opening* is the space between the tip of the reed and the tip of the mouthpiece.
- The *facing length* is the distance from the tip opening to where the reed first touches the mouthpiece. It's not just the length of the facing (or *lay*) which matters, but its curvature too.

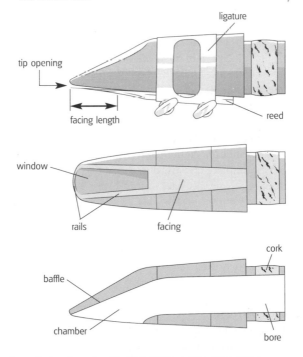

A mouthpiece from the side, from below and in cross-section

- The opening which is closed off by the reed is called the *window* or *windcut*. Behind the window is the *chamber*.
- The other end, where the mouthpiece connects with the barrel, is the *bore*.

Numbers or words

Mouthpiece brochures usually tell you exactly how big the tip opening and facing length of each mouthpiece are. On their own, those figures don't tell you too much because a mouthpiece has many more dimensions which affect its performance. So it's usually more useful to read what a brochure says about the sound you can make with a mouthpiece and the type of music it is designed for. A subdued sound, for instance, can be good for some types of chamber music – just as a sound that blends well might be ideal for symphonic work. Lots of volume and projection may be useful for orchestras that play outdoors, but jazz players may prefer a mouthpiece offering lots of flexibility.

Different brand, different sound

Each mouthpiece manufacturer has its own 'character'. While one brand's mouthpieces may sound quite direct, those of another might be warmer in tone. As ever, though, which is better depends on who you ask.

Easy

Some clarinettists spend their whole lives looking for the ideal mouthpiece. Others are much less demanding, or they have an 'easy embouchure' – meaning that exactly which mouthpiece they use doesn't matter nearly as much. Such players generally have less problems with reeds, too.

One or more

Similarly, there are clarinettists who use one and the same mouthpiece for all kinds of musical styles, and others who select from two, three or more different mouthpieces, each with its own character.

German on French

German clarinets have very different mouthpieces to French ones, with smaller tip openings and longer facings. The reed is usually not attached with a ligature but bound on with a cord. If you fit a German mouthpiece to a French clarinet, you'll immediately hear how much influence the mouthpiece has on the sound: it makes a French clarinet sound very 'German'. Some clarinettists always use that particular combination – but this may mean modifying the mouthpiece or barrel slightly.

Buying a mouthpiece

If you are going out to choose a new mouthpiece, the following tips may be of use:

- It's good to know roughly **what you're looking for**. Then a decent salesperson will be able to recommend just a handful of mouthpieces, to save you trying hundreds.
- Take **your own clarinet and mouthpiece with you** for comparison.
- If you always use a **mouthpiece cushion** (see page 70), don't test other mouthpieces without one. Using a mouthpiece cushion will also prevent you leaving tooth marks in new mouthpieces.
- Don't compare twenty different mouthpieces at once. Instead, **choose three**, listen, and replace the worst one with another. And so on.
- Take regular **breaks**: after fifteen minutes of testing you won't be able to hear what you're doing nearly as well.
- Choosing the perfect mouthpiece in one go is difficult because you only really get to know a new mouthpiece **after a few weeks' playing**.
- A mouthpiece won't perform to its full potential until you have found the right reed to go with it. A good salesperson can advise you on good **reed/mouthpiece combinations**.
- When you are testing mouthpieces, be sure to always use a **good, new reed**.
- When it comes to mouthpieces, **hundredths of millimetres** often make a difference. That's why no two mouthpieces are the same. Even if you know exactly which type you want, it's still worth trying out a few similar ones: there's a good chance you'll find one you prefer.

THE DIFFERENCES

How a mouthpiece plays and sounds depends on the tip opening, the length and curvature of the facing, the material and much else besides.

Names and numbers

Almost all manufacturers use combinations of letters and numbers to identify their different mouthpieces. Sadly, those 'codes' usually tell you nothing. For example, with one brand a higher number means a larger tip opening, but with another it means precisely the opposite.

Almost the same, but very different

The Vandoren B45 is one popular mouthpiece, and two others that resemble it are the Leblanc L4 and the Selmer 120 – but you wouldn't know that if you only looked at the codes. Only a few brands advertise the information you really need: the dimensions of the tip, the facing and the chamber on their mouthpieces.

Comparing

But on the Internet and at good clarinet shops you can find tables listing the characteristics of mouthpieces by different brands side by side. These can make your quest a lot easier.

The whole thing

Everything to do with mouthpieces is interrelated. This means that two mouthpieces with the same tip opening and the same facing length may nevertheless sound and play very differently. Or one of them may work brilliantly on one clarinet or for one clarinettist, and terribly on another. In the end, it's a matter of trying them out until you find the perfect combination: when clarinet, mouthpiece, reed, barrel and ligature together sound and play exactly the way you want them to.

TIP OPENING

When it comes to tip openings, hundredths or even thousandths of an inch really do count. Most French mouthpieces have openings of between 0.039" and 0.047" (1–1.2mm), and this range – tiny though it is – can make a great deal of difference.

Beginners and all-rounders

Many beginners choose a mouthpiece with a tip opening of around 0.045"; not too big (because then you would need to correct the pitch too much) and not too small (because you'd need too much air). A versatile mouthpiece which suits clarinettists in all kinds of different styles is likely to have a similar, medium-sized tip opening.

Small
A smaller tip opening produces more resistance and a darker sound, and also requires a softer reed. A tip opening of this size is potentially quite hard work: the reed doesn't move as far, so the pitch and sound are not as easy to correct, and if the opening is too small, the sound becomes too dull, the pitch becomes too high and you have to blow very hard.

Large
A large tip opening makes blowing easier, giving more volume and a more vivid and open sound. There's a lot of scope for correcting pitch and tone, allowing you to slide from note to note, for instance. But the fact that you *can* correct more also means you *always have to* correct more. With a large tip opening you need a hard reed. The biggest tip opening is just under 0.059" (1.5mm) – but such extreme mouthpieces are rare.

Converting
Tip openings are often given in hundredths of a millimetre – a 125 tip opening is actually 1.25mm, or 1.25/25.4 = 0.049". American brands tend to use thousandths of an inch: a size 50 would be 0.050", or 0.050 x 25.4 = 1.27mm.

Other clarinets
Mouthpieces for larger and smaller clarinets naturally have larger and smaller tip openings respectively. To give you an idea, the tip opening of a bass clarinet mouthpiece is usually somewhere between 0.060" and 0.080" (1.5–2mm).

THE FACING
On its own, the facing length doesn't tell you very much – it's the combination of the facing length and the tip opening which is really important. A small tip opening with a long facing, for instance, gives a good response with

a dark, rich tone. But if you combine that same facing length with a large tip opening, you will get a brighter tone and more volume.

Curvature and facing

At least as important as the length of the facing is its curvature – but the brochures often tell you next to nothing about it. The main reason is that it is not easy to describe how 'curved' a facing is. The facing (length and curvature) and the tip opening, which are closely related, are in fact sometimes collectively called the *facing*. So a mouthpiece with an *all-purpose facing* has a medium-sized tip opening and a medium-length facing that is neither too curved nor too flat.

Long or short

On French mouthpieces, the facing length varies between about 0.710" and 0.865" (18–22mm). A longer facing allows you to make a broader, bigger sound; a shorter facing is more likely to produce a more focused sound.

Words or letters

The facing length is often indicated using words or letters rather than numbers. But beware – what one brand calls short, another brand may call medium.

The edges

The edges of the mouthpiece are also part of the facing. If the left- and right-hand edges are not exactly the same

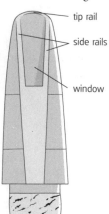

tip rail

side rails

window

shape and thickness, the mouthpiece will be 'out of balance'. As a result you may get squeaks, or your instrument may have a poor response or a shrill sound.

Sound

The thickness of the edges (the *side rails* and *tip rail*) also affects the tone. Thicker edges make the sound thicker and darker, thin edges give a brighter sound. If the edges are too thick, the sound becomes dull; if they are too thin it becomes shrill.

CHAMBER, BAFFLE, BORE AND TABLE

A mouthpiece with a large chamber will produce a dark, warm, full sound which is especially well-suited to classical music. For a bright, vivid sound with a good projection, you're better off with a mouthpiece that has a smaller chamber.

Baffle

Some mouthpieces have a so-called *baffle* (see illustration on page 63). This lowering of the chamber's 'ceiling' (the *palate*) compresses the air, making the sound more vivid and edgy. Conversely, a concave palate makes the sound darker.

Bore

There are special mouthpieces for instruments with large or narrow bores, but you don't usually need to pay special attention to the bore of the mouthpiece itself. But if you're interested, the mouthpiece bore has a comparable effect to the bore of the instrument: a narrow bore gives a tighter, more focused, darker sound, and a wide bore a 'wider', more open sound.

Table

The table, which the reed sits upon, is usually flat, though on some mouthpieces it's a tiny bit concave when looked at lengthways. This slight depression in the table is supposed to allow the reed to vibrate more freely, which in turn enables you to influence the sound a little more – whether by the tension of your lips or by your choice of ligature.

Beaks and bites

Mouthpieces differ in many other ways – the *beak angle* may vary, for instance. That means that the part you set your teeth on is either steeper or less steep than normal, making the mouthpiece feel either fatter or thinner. There are also mouthpieces which have been specially adapted for clarinettists who have teeth that overbite or underbite.

MATERIALS

Most clarinet mouthpieces are made of ebonite (hardened rubber), but they can also be made of plastic, crystal, metal, wood or other materials.

Ebonite

Ebonite mouthpieces tend to offer a fairly warm, dark sound, but there are some which can make your sound quite edgy. This difference is partly down to the hardness of the ebonite and partly to the shape of the mouthpiece.

Wear

One problem with ebonite is that it wears in time. One cause of wear is cleaning; another is that the reed constantly beats the mouthpiece when you play: a clarinet has what is technically known as a *beating reed*. So if you're finding it very hard to find a reed that works with your instrument, or if your tone is growing shrill and harsh, try a different mouthpiece – you may find that yours is worn out.

Plastic

Plastic is mainly (but not exclusively) used for cheap mouthpieces. The sound is often harder and brighter than ebonite.

Crystal, glass and metal

Most crystal mouthpieces are made to give a dark, warm sound, but some actually sound brighter. Crystal is very fragile, but on the plus side it doesn't wear as quickly as ebonite. Glass and metal mouthpieces are fairly rare.

Wood

A wooden mouthpiece makes most clarinets sound extra dark and round. Because no two pieces of wood are the same, there can be a lot of variation between two 'identical' mouthpieces. Wooden mouthpieces also react quickly to changes in temperature and humidity.

MOUTHPIECE CUSHIONS

Most clarinettists use mouthpiece cushions on their mouthpieces. These protect both the mouthpiece from your teeth and your teeth from the vibration of the mouthpiece. Their soft synthetic material also gives you a bit of extra grip on the mouthpiece.

Bright

A mouthpiece cushion can even affect the sound – especially the sound as you hear it yourself, because less noise is

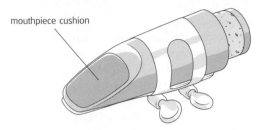

mouthpiece cushion

A mouthpiece cushion makes you sound and play differently

transmitted directly through your teeth. A mouthpiece cushion makes you open your mouth a fraction further, often changing the sound still more. Mouthpiece cushions come in different thicknesses and hardnesses, and some brands adhere better than others. Try a few different ones and decide which one you like best – they're not expensive. You can buy them individually or in sets.

GERMAN MOUTHPIECES

German mouthpieces have a much smaller tip opening (approximately 0.025–0.040" or 0.65–1mm) than French ones, and a longer facing length (from around 0.730"–0.985" or 18.5–25mm, or even more).

Window and walls

The window is also narrower than on a French mouthpiece. If you look through a German mouthpiece, you'll see that the side walls get slightly further apart towards the end. These *angled side walls* are said to make the sound, which is focused by the narrow window, a bit broader. Straight side walls, on the other hand, are said to enhance the projection and make the sound less warm.

Cord

The ligature of German mouthpieces is different too. German clarinettists still often bind their reeds to the mouthpiece with a cord. In order to give the cord some grip, the mouthpiece has grooves all around it.

MOUTHPIECE BRANDS

There are many mouthpiece brands. Vandoren, which also makes reeds, is the biggest. Most clarinet brands also have their own mouthpieces, but often they don't actually manufacture them in-house. Ernst Schreiber is just one example of a manufacturer that makes mouthpieces for lots of other companies (as well as producing mouthpieces under its own ESM brand). Most other manufacturers are small firms that produce expensive handmade mouthpieces: Charles Bay, Brilhart, Gigliotti, Hite, Piet Jeegers, Lakey, Pomarico and Woodwind are some examples. Mouthpieces with a Viotto facing are made in Germany. Many small brands finish mouthpieces which are supplied already cut into their basic shape by the Zinner firm.

BARRELS

The barrel or *socket* is primarily used to alter the tuning of the clarinet (which is why it is sometimes called the *tuning barrel*), but it also has a significant influence on the sound, intonation and how easy it is to play.

Two barrels

Many professional quality clarinets come with two barrels, one of them one or two millimetres longer than the other. The longer barrel makes the instrument sound just a little lower (flatter); the shorter one makes it a fraction higher (sharper).

Shorter higher, longer lower

You might use that shorter barrel if you were playing with an orchestra that tunes slightly higher, or if it's very cold and your instrument is sounding a bit too low. Some clarinettists play slightly lower than others, even with exactly the same instrument, mouthpiece and reed, so it might also be useful for them. And if you buy a mouthpiece that sounds just a little higher or lower, a longer or shorter barrel can make sure that your tuning still remains accurate.

Preferably longer

Some clarinettists prefer to play with the longest barrel they can use while still staying in tune, because they say even those one or two millimetres make their sound just a little deeper and warmer.

Too long, too short

The length of the barrel has a greater effect on the pitch of the notes from the upper part of the clarinet (the short-tube notes) than on the other notes. So if you choose a barrel which is too long, those short-tube notes will become much too low compared to the other notes. If your barrel is too short, on the other hand, the short-tube notes will be too high compared to the others. Barrels can be too long or too short even if they differ from the original barrel by some 0.060" (1.5mm).

Adjustable

Adjustable barrels are also available. They usually range from approximately 2.365" to 3.150" (60–80mm) in length. But of course, you can only use about 0.120" (3mm) of that range before the barrel becomes either too long or too short to still play in tune.

Thick and thin

Separate barrels come not only in different lengths but also in different thicknesses and materials, and with different bores. A barrel with a thicker wall gives a darker, heavier, fuller sound. A clarinet with a

A barrel which can be adjusted millimetre by millimetre
(Click Tuning Barrel).

thin-walled barrel responds more easily and has a brighter, lighter sound.

Material

Cheaper wooden clarinets sometimes have a bell and a barrel made of plastic. If you replace the barrel with a wooden one, the sound can noticeably improve. Besides barrels made of grenadilla, you can also get all kinds of unusual designs in bronze and special varieties of wood, or wooden barrels lined with ebonite for a somewhat brighter sound.

Bore

The bore is also important. Barrels with cylindrical bores sound more open and wider than barrels whose bores get steadily narrower towards the bottom. This *reverse taper* produces a more focused, warmer sound. There are many other variations, each of which have their own effect on the sound, the intonation (especially that of the short-tube notes) and the response of the instrument. Some barrels even have interchangeable bores.

Hard to predict
Exactly how any specific barrel will behave is difficult to predict: it depends to a large extent on how you play, your mouthpiece, the reed and of course the instrument itself.

Brands
Each clarinet brand makes its own barrels. In addition, there are a few specialized brands, of which Chadash and Moennig are the best known.

NECKS
Larger clarinets, such as the alto and the bass, have a metal neck instead of a barrel. This neck is used to tune the instrument. Some necks consist of two sections which you fix together with a screw. Other types use cork tenons like an ordinary clarinet. Some brands supply one shorter and one longer neck to go with each instrument, just as you sometimes get two barrels with an ordinary clarinet.

From the front
When you play a bass clarinet, the mouthpiece enters your mouth at a different angle to that of an ordinary clarinet: from the front instead of from below. That can make things difficult for clarinettists who play both instruments and often need to swap between them. That's why some bass clarinet necks are bent in such a way that the mouthpiece enters your mouth a little closer to the vertical.

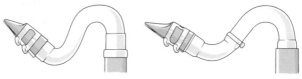

ordinary neck   neck with modified crook

With the special neck (right), the mouthpiece enters your mouth at a different angle

LIGATURES

Even the ligature contributes to your sound. The differences lie mainly in the material that it's made of and how the reed is held in place.

One or two

Many ligatures have two screws. Although this takes a little more work to tighten each time, it does ensure a good distribution of pressure across the reed. Other ligatures do the same job with a single screw.

Inverted

An *inverted* ligature has screws not at the bottom of the mouthpiece but on top of it. This supposedly allows the reed to move more freely and so respond more easily.

Material

Besides conventional metal ligatures, there are models in leather, soft plastic, textile or woven metal thread. The softer and thicker the material, the darker and more velvety the sound sometimes becomes. The same happens if you secure the reed with a cord, as many German clarinettists do. A 'soft' ligature of this kind is also said to make the sound more flexible and deeper.

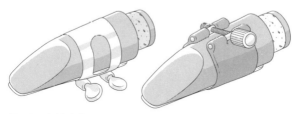

Metal and fabric ligatures

Spots or strips

A very different effect is produced if the reed is held in place only by a few raised metal spots or thin, metal strips. The theory is that the less material there is touching the reed, the more freely it can vibrate; this usually makes the sound brighter and more open, and encourages the instrument to respond more easily. Other ligatures have adjustable clamp systems, so that you can adapt the sound to the music you are playing, the room you are in or the kind of ensemble you're part of.

Tips and tricks

You can also adjust simple ligatures to some extent. If you have a reed which is too light, tighten the upper screw a bit less. That allows a longer section of the reed to vibrate, which has the same effect as a slightly heavier reed. You can read more tips and tricks in Chapter 8, *Before and After*.

Bite

Another point to watch out for: some types of ligature allow you to vary the exact position of the reed very easily, even without (re)moving the ligature itself. Others don't. Another difference is that some ligatures 'bite' into the reed. This means that you'll only be able to fix the reed in that same position from then on.

Prices

A simple ligature costs around £5, but you can easily pay twice as much or still more for special models. Almost all clarinet and mouthpiece brands have their own ligatures, and in addition there are also specialist brands such as B&G, Rovner, Oleg and Winslow. Remember that a different ligature usually needs a different *cap* to protect it, so if the new ligature doesn't come with one you'll have to get a replacement.

7. REEDS

What strings are to guitarists and violinists, reeds are to clarinettists. They greatly affect the way you play, giving you a lot of flexibility about the kind of sound you make. But you have to replace them frequently and it can sometimes be difficult to find a good reed, so they can be a bit of a pain too. The good news is that there are lots of tricks to make a decent reed last as long as possible.

The most immediate difference between reeds is their stiffness. The softest reeds are used mainly by beginners and on mouthpieces with narrow tip openings. To use a hard reed, which you'll find especially on mouthpieces with large tip openings, you need to be able to play well. You can tell how hard or soft a reed is by its number.

Numbers

Most manufacturers rate their reeds on a scale of 1 to 5, often in half steps. The higher the number, the stiffer or harder the reed.

Harders

A harder reed gives a heavier, darker, thicker or fuller sound, and makes playing softly and low more difficult. It's not as easy to correct the pitch when playing with a hard reed – but this also means that playing louder or softer will not result in pitch variations that easily.

Softer

If you use a softer reed, there is a greater chance that the pitch will go up and down. A soft reed speaks more easily and gives a bright, lighter sound, and makes playing softly easier.

Equally thick
A higher number simply means that the reed is harder, being cut from a less flexible piece of cane. It will be exactly the same thickness as a reed with a lower number, assuming it's the same type of reed.

Different brands
What one manufacturer calls a 2 may be equivalent to a 1½ or a 2½ reed from another brand. The actual stiffness indicated by the number can even vary for different series by the same brand. And some brands use words – soft, medium, hard, etc – instead of numbers to describe the hardness of their reeds. As with mouthpieces, there are tables you can consult which list all kinds of brands and series side by side.

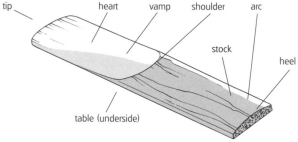

A reed consists of countless hollow miniature tubes, as can be seen at the tip

In a box
When you buy a box of reeds it will nearly always contain some reeds that are good, some that are less good and others which are poor. If boxes consistently seem to be lacking in decent reeds, try a different brand or a different type – and be sure that the problem doesn't lie somewhere else. If your mouthpiece is crooked or damaged, for instance, you'll have problems with any reed.

Not equally hard
Of course, ten 'identical' reeds from one and the same box won't all be equally stiff either. Some will be a little softer or more flexible, others a little harder.

Higher, steeper, brighter

How a reed plays and sounds also depends on its shape. The thickness of the *heart* may be greater or less great, the slope towards the edges may be a little steeper or a little more gentle, and so on. For example, you can buy reeds which are cut a little thicker and make the sound a little tighter and clearer, with more 'core' to the tone.

French file cut

Reeds with a *French file cut* have an extra part of the bark removed, making the sound somewhat brighter and more flexible, and allowing the reed to speak more easily. This enhances the flexibility of the reed, making for an easier response, especially in the low register. It also helps produce a brighter, more narrowly focused sound. The French file cut is also called *file cut* or *double cut*, while the 'regular' or *unfiled cut* is sometimes referred to as *single cut*.

Which brand

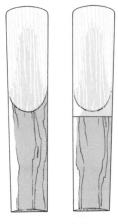

Each brand makes different types of reeds. The only way to find out which reed you like best is to keep trying them out. Trading experiences with other clarinettists helps, but every clarinettist blows differently, and a reed which works brilliantly with one mouthpiece can be hopeless on another.

Reeds without (left) and with (right) a French file cut

Still looking

If you're still looking for reeds that suit you, buy lots of different series, brands and numbers. Try more than one reed of each type: one bad reed tells you nothing. Most clarinettists who have found 'their' reed buy them in boxes of five or ten. Reeds usually cost 70p–£2 each.

German and Austrian reeds

The reeds used for a German mouthpiece are cut differently to French reeds: they have a different *profile*. You often read that you shouldn't use German reeds on a

French mouthpiece, or the other way around – but some clarinettists are very enthusiastic about such combinations. There are also special mouthpieces and reeds for Austrian (Viennese) players.

LOOKING AND PLAYING

There are all kinds of ways to discover whether a reed is good or not, and there are all kinds of tricks to make reeds last as long as possible.

Against the light

If you hold up a reed to the light, you'll see an inverted 'V' shape. That V must be precisely in the centre, and the reed must get thinner evenly to the left and to the right. 'Crooked' reeds squeak and don't blow comfortably.

| Good V-shape: may sound good | A 'crooked' reed: risk of squeaks | Uneven grain: better not to buy it | Knots: may vibrate unevenly |

Too young

A good reed is golden yellow to golden brown in colour. Reeds with a hint of green are too young: they won't play well, if at all, and won't last long.

Grain and knots

An even grain is more likely to sound good than a grain which crosses the reed at different angles. Reeds which have spots and knots on the sanded area are unlikely to vibrate evenly.

Wet it first

You won't know how good a reed really is until you have

been playing with it for a while. Dry reeds don't vibrate properly, so always wet your reed first. Do so by keeping it in your mouth for thirty seconds or so or placing it in a glass of lukewarm water. The latter method may extend the life of a reed: water is thought to be better for reeds than saliva – but, of course, there are players who disagree.

Break them in

Reeds which perform very well straight away often don't last very long. The best reeds are often the ones which seem a little hard to begin with – in other words, they don't initially play especially well. That's why some clarinettists first 'break in' their new reeds, for instance by only using them a few minutes per day for the first week. They may also use that breaking-in period to adjust the reed if necessary – a little bit every day. Other clarinettists regard that as nonsense: if a reed doesn't play well, they simply move on to the next one.

Double plus, double minus

When you're testing a box of new reeds, give each reed a grade, or give the best reeds two plus marks and the worst ones two minuses and so on. Don't throw away the 'bad' reeds straight away, but leave them for a few months: sometimes they will improve by themselves, and they never get too old. You can also try adjusting the poorer ones (see page 82).

Swapping

Some people say reeds last longer if you don't use the same one for too long at a stretch. Indeed, some clarinettists always have a supply of good reeds on them so that they can switch reeds every hour or half an hour. Another reason to alternate reeds regularly is that otherwise your reed will gradually become weaker and by the time the reed finally 'goes', it will be so weak that any new reed you try will seem very hard.

Suddenly

If you change reeds regularly, you will also get a better feel for the little differences between reeds. What's more, you'll always have plenty of good reeds to hand – which is useful, because even the best reed can 'go' suddenly.

Big differences

You can also deliberately use those differences between reeds: for example, you can choose a softer-playing reed if the air is very dry, or if the acoustics are dead, and a slightly harder reed if the air is very humid, or if you are playing a venue with a large echo, like a church. There are even clarinettists who always carry a range of reeds to suit every possible occasion.

A matter of taste

If you don't like the taste of cane, you could try some flavoured reeds, or get a bottle of reed flavouring, which is available in various tastes.

ADJUSTING REEDS

Some clarinettists adjust every reed themselves, others do so only if it is really necessary. Learning to adjust reeds takes a lot of time and, to start with, a lot of reeds. A few important tips are listed below; on pages 131–132 you'll find the titles of a number of books which discuss this subject at greater length.

Higher, lower or crooked

Before you start adjusting a reed, first experiment with its exact position on the mouthpiece. A reed which doesn't seem to work or work well when it is perfectly straight may suddenly start sounding good if you mount it a little higher, a little lower or at a slight angle – in which case adjustment will no longer be necessary. Want to know more? See page 89.

Flat

If you have a reed whose *facing* (the part in contact with the mouthpiece) is not perfectly flat, you can sand it down. Lay a piece of very fine sandpaper (number 320 or finer) on a small plate of glass to make sure it is level, and draw the reed across it a few times. You can also use a whetstone or carborundum stone instead. Carefully turn the reed, first clockwise, then anticlockwise. Exert as little pressure as possible and don't let the tip touch the stone. Some people scour the reed with a sharp penknife instead, pulling the blade across the reed sideways a few times.

Too soft

A reed which is too soft can 'shut off' the sound completely, or leave you with a messy, unsteady tone. The solution is to clip off 1–1.5mm (0.04–0.06") from the tip with a *reed cutter* or *reed trimmer*, but make sure you wet the reed first. You may need to file off the corners a little after cutting. Always do so towards the centre of the reed, and only if it is necessary. Reed cutters cost around £30.

Too hard

If a reed is too hard, you can make it more flexible by scraping it with a sharp knife or a piece of Dutch rush, which you can buy in some music shops. Start in the area marked figure 1 in the illustration, but do so carefully, because the reed is already very thin at this point. If necessary, go on to the areas marked 2, then to 3 and 4. Always remove equal amounts left and right, otherwise you'll push the reed out of balance.

Shrill or dull

You can try rescuing a reed which sounds shrill by adjusting the areas marked 3 and 4, but it's not an easy job. On reeds that sound dull you start at 1 and move on to 3 and 4, and possibly 2 as well.

Squeaking

Squeaking reeds are often not equally flexible or equally thick on the left and right. In the latter case, you can try making the thicker edge a little thinner. Keep checking how much you have removed by fitting the reed to the mouthpiece and blowing at an angle in your mouth, comparing left and right.

Tips

- Work carefully: it's easy to remove **too much material**. Taking as little as one hundredth of a millimetre from the tip of a reed makes it a whole ten percent thinner.
- Check **how much you have removed** as you work. Instead of constantly taking the ligature off and putting it back on again, you can also hold the reed in place with your thumb.

- If there are **crinkles** at the tip of the reed, don't tear it. They will naturally go down when you start playing, or if you briefly put the reed in a glass of water.
- Some reeds will **never be any good**, however much you work on them.
- Avoid the area marked X, the **heart of the reed**.
- If you really want to tackle the job properly, you can buy a special **reed adjustment device**. In Germany, and especially in Austria, many clarinettists still make their reeds themselves.

LIFETIME

A reed consists of countless hollow miniature tubes or fibres with a soft material called *pith* between them. The pith becomes gradually softer from exposure to your saliva, until it gets so soft that the reed stops working altogether. How long that takes depends on the type of saliva you have, how often you play and on the reed itself. Reeds often last between two and four weeks, but there is one clarinettist who claims to have been playing with the same reed for thirteen years: he only uses it when he performs Mozart in the summer . . .

Tips

There are all kinds of ways in which you can try to increase the useful life of your reeds.

- Rinse your reed **in clean water** after playing. Then dry it, for instance with a cotton cloth or handkerchief, or by passing it between your thumb and index finger, always towards the tip. Some clarinet players just dry the reed without rinsing it first.
- Always store your reeds in a good **reed guard** (see page 93).
- Lay each new reed on a flat surface and firmly rub it from the thick end to the thin end with the back of a teaspoon. This **closes the fibres** in the reed, so enhancing its life expectancy.
- **Don't play too long in one go** with the same reed (see page 81).
- **Break your reeds in**, so that the dried material gradually gets used to being wet again.
- **Hydrogen peroxide** solution (3 percent, available from

your local pharmacy) counteracts the effect of your saliva on the reed. Put your reeds in the solution overnight once in a while, and rinse them well before you use them again.

· **Taking a break?** A mouthpiece cap protects your reed and keeps it moist.

Plastic reeds

Plastic or synthetic reeds are also available, for example from the brands BARI, Fiberreed, Fibracell, Hahn and Légère. They are a good deal more expensive but they do last much longer and they are very consistent: two 'identical' plastic reeds really are identical. They are also useful if you play different clarinets during a concert, as you don't need to wet them first. Many players feel that plastic reeds tend to sound shrill, harsh or edgy, but they are relatively new and being improved all the time. Besides plastic reeds, reeds with a plastic layer around them, such as Rico Plasticovers, are also available.

Reed brands

The American Rico company also makes reeds sold under the brands LaVoz and Mitchell Lurie. The firms Brancher, Glotin, Marca, Rigotti, Selmer (which also makes clarinets) and Vandoren (which also makes mouthpieces) are from France, which is where most of the reed cane is grown. Some other brand names are Alexander Superial (Japan), Vintage Reeds (Australia), RKM and Zonda.

8. BEFORE AND AFTER

This chapter covers all the things you need to do to your clarinet before and after playing: from putting it together and warming it up to tuning it, taking it apart, drying and storing it. It also includes tips on amplification, stands and lyres. Serious maintenance is dealt with in Chapter 9.

Wooden clarinets can crack due to rapid changes in temperature and humidity. If you've been outdoors on a very cold day and you then walk into a warm room, you should allow your clarinet to acclimatize in its case first. You can also warm it up in your hands. Don't start playing until the instrument no longer feels cold to the touch, so that the moisture and warmth of your breath won't shock the material.

Only one way
There's usually only one way to put a clarinet back into its case, but exactly how it fits depends on the case – so take a good look at how the clarinet is positioned inside before taking it out. Be especially careful with the upper and lower joints to avoid bending the keys.

Cork grease
Cork grease is wonderful stuff: it makes everything slide more smoothly when you're putting your clarinet together, it keeps the cork in good condition for longer and seals the joints more effectively. It comes either in small pots or in a lipstick-style container to stop you getting it on your fingers. Apple-scented cork grease and other 'flavours' are also available.

Upper joint

There are all kinds of ways to assemble a clarinet. One common method is described below. A tip before you start: never lift the upper and lower joints out of the case by the keywork. Use a finger to lift them up a little by one end so that you can then get hold of them properly.

Bell on lower joint

First pick up the lower joint. Hold it as shown in the illustration and then attach the bell with a careful twisting movement.

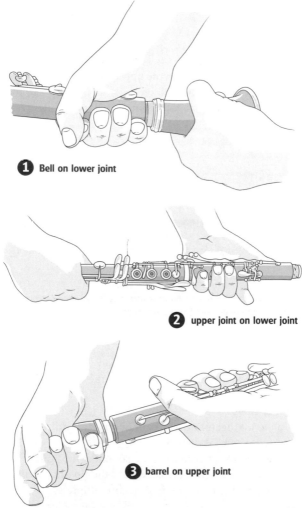

1 Bell on lower joint

2 upper joint on lower joint

3 barrel on upper joint

Upper joint on lower joint

Now take hold of the upper joint, resting your fingers on the rings. Press those rings down as you attach the upper joint to the lower joint with a careful twisting movement. Hold the lower joint at the bottom end, as shown in the illustration, without squeezing the mechanism. The bell will give you extra grip.

The bridge

To avoid damaging the bridge mechanism, it should be in the 'open' position when you're joining the upper and lower joints together. That means pressing down the rings of the upper joint and *not* pressing down the rings of the lower joint.

Barrel on upper joint

Now slide the barrel onto the upper joint. The easiest way to do this is to rest the bell on the top of your leg so that you don't have to grip the clarinet itself too tightly.

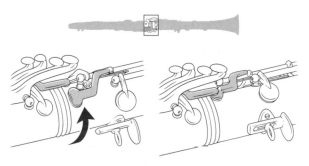

Hold down the D/A ring so that the bridge is in the open position as you slide the upper and lower joints together

Mouthpiece

Again, rest the bell against your leg to help you slide the mouthpiece onto the barrel. Next, fit the reed.

In four steps

1. Slide the ligature over the mouthpiece until it almost reaches its final position.
2. Place the wetted reed (see page 80) under the ligature . . .
3. . . . and make sure the edges and the tip are exactly in line with the rails and tip of the mouthpiece.

4. Now slide the ligature into place and tighten it. Not too tightly, though, otherwise the reed won't vibrate properly.

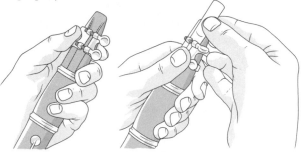

1 First the ligature...   **2 ... then the reed**

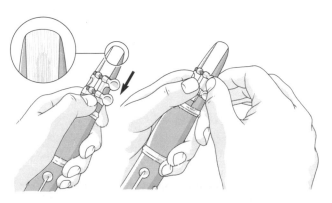

3 Check its position...   **4 ... then tighten the ligature**

If a reed is hard to play, you can set it a little lower down the mouthpiece. If it feels very light, try moving it up a bit, or sliding the ligature down slightly, or loosening the upper screw a little. Reeds which are not perfectly even left and right will often perform better if you set them on your mouthpiece at a slight angle.

In line

The mouthpiece, the upper and the lower joints must all be in line. From the front you can usually tell by looking at the brand name if it's shown on all the joints. Or you can look along the underside of the instrument, from the bell to the reed. A few brands have special catches to make sure the upper and lower joints are always in line.

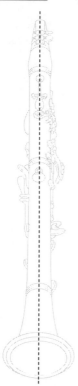

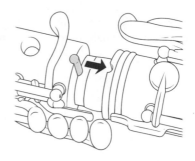

This special catch keeps both joints in line
(LeBlanc)

Brushing and flossing, food and drink

If you want to make it as easy as possible to keep your clarinet clean, wash your hands before you play. It's also a good idea to brush and floss your teeth, and don't eat or consume sugary drinks between sessions.

TUNING

Is everything in line? Look along the underside of the instrument

Like most other instruments, a clarinet needs to be tuned before you start playing. The usual method of adjusting tuning is to pull the upper joint and barrel apart by one or two millimetres (0.04–0.08"), but this obviously makes the sound lower – not much use if you're already too low. Some players get round this by using a shorter barrel, but if you don't have one try warming your clarinet up – cold instruments nearly always sound too low.

To A

Most orchestras and bands tune to a sounding A (concert pitch A). On a B flat clarinet that means you play a B. The cheapest way of producing a reliable sounding A is to use a tuning fork – a thick metal fork which you tap against your knee before holding next to your ear to hear the note. Tuning forks are also available in other tunings (see pages 38–39). Electronic tuners and metronomes can often produce this A note, too. If you have a piano or a keyboard handy, the A you want is just to the right of the centre.

A tuning fork

To other notes

In some cases you may want or need to tune to other notes. In concert bands you may have to use C (sounding B flat), because many brass instruments are also pitched in B flat. Other alternatives are the open G (sounding F) or the D (sounding C), because both are thought to be more stable than the B on the clarinet.

Barrel and upper joint

Often tuning is simply a matter of adjusting how close the barrel and the upper joint are to each other. But that isn't always enough, because when you pull the barrel and upper joints apart, the short-tube notes go down further than the long-tube notes, just as they would if you were to use a longer barrel (see pages 72–74).

The rest

If you also pull apart the upper and lower joints slightly, the notes which go down the most are the highest notes of the lower joint. By pulling out the bell a little, you can fine-tune the long-tube notes a tiny bit.

Different notes

Because each clarinet has certain notes which tend to sound too low and others which tend to sound too high, you should never tune to just one note. For instance, if you tune to an open G, you might try also playing the higher and lower E and B notes (the notes of the E minor chord), and listening to whether the distances between those notes are correct. If you are tuning to a C, you could also play the E and G (the C major chord).

Groove

When you pull two sections of a clarinet apart, you'll notice that a groove lies between them – not just on the outside, but also on the inside of the bore. If the gap is too wide, these grooves can cause the sound to deteriorate. Moreover, condensation easily collects in them and they heighten the effects of tuning: when you pull the barrel out, the short-tube notes become even more obviously too low.

Tuning rings

One solution is to use *tuning rings*, which you place inside the tenons so that they fill up the grooves on the inside. Tuning rings are usually sold in sets of three, with thicknesses such as 0.5, 1.0 and 2.0 millimetres. A set like this should only cost you a few pounds. Some clarinettists swear by tuning rings, but most players don't use them, because the rings need to be taken out if you want to tune to a higher pitch and because they sometimes buzz when you play low notes.

Tuners

An electronic tuner can be useful when tuning your clarinet. Its built-in microphone 'hears' the note you're playing and tells you whether the pitch is too high (sharp), too low (flat) or exactly right. Special tuners for transposing instruments such as the clarinet are available. Simply move the switch and the tuner shifts to the key of your instrument, so that when you play a B flat it shows a B flat, rather than the sounding pitch C.

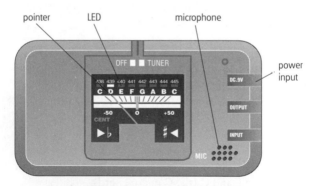

A chromatic tuner shows you which note it 'hears'

Hotter means higher

After you've been playing for a while your instrument will gradually warm up. This makes the tuning go up too, so that after five to ten minutes' playing you'll often need to retune slightly.

AFTER

If you never clean your clarinet, you'll notice that your mouthpiece starts smelling funny. And that's not the only thing that can go wrong.

Reed

Reeds last longest if you rinse them and then dry them after playing (see page 84). If you leave your reed on the mouthpiece, it won't dry as easily, which will make it more likely to warp. Besides, you'll have to take it off to wet it next time you play anyway.

Reed guards

Reed guards come in countless varieties, from simple plastic holders to deluxe leather-clad boxes, and with prices ranging from £2 to £30. Your reeds will dry most evenly in a reed guard with ventilation holes and a ribbed floor, so that the air can get to every part. Other boxes have glass floors which help to prevent crinkles forming at the tip of the reed.

Cartridges

You can also get reed guards with replaceable cartridges containing a substance that keeps the humidity at exactly the right level. Reeds can go mouldy if you keep them in a case which is completely closed. Simple holders for two or more reeds only cost a pound or two.

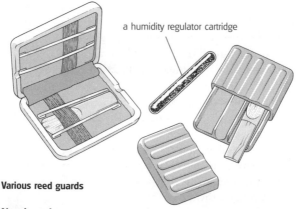

a humidity regulator cartridge

Various reed guards

Numbered

Some reed guards have numbered compartments so you can tell the reeds apart. This is specially useful for clarinettists who change reeds constantly or who use different reeds for different situations.

Drying
Before you put your clarinet away, you need to dry it: it's better for the wood and for the pads. Ideally, take the mouthpiece off and give the reed a quick rinse in lukewarm water before you dry it, perhaps with a handkerchief.

Swabs
Next dry the rest of the clarinet with a *swab* or *pull-through*: a cloth with a cord and a weight attached to it. Lower the swab through the clarinet weight-first, and then pull it back up through the instrument.

From the bell upwards
The barrel is the part that gets the wettest, so it seems logical to pull the cloth through the instrument from the bell upwards. All the same, some clarinettists prefer to do it the other way round (or both), and some even dry their instruments joint by joint. If you decide to do it that way, take the clarinet apart, lay the parts safely in your case and take them out again one by one to dry them.

Register tube
A swab can get caught behind the register tube or the thumb tube. Free it by pulling it back a little way in the other direction.

Tenons, toneholes and pads
Don't forget to dry the tenons. Condensation often collects there, as it does in the tone-holes. If you have wet toneholes, your pads won't make seal properly. Sometimes you can dry toneholes simply by blowing on them from the outside. Otherwise, blow hard through the lower or upper joint. Dry wet pads with a cigarette paper (see pages 96).

Dry your clarinet with a pull-through swab

Cotton or chamois

Most swabs have cotton cloths, but some are made of chamois leather or silk. Cotton cloths need to be washed regularly, even when they are new: new cotton doesn't dry as well as old. Chamois leather, on the other hand, should never be washed.

Padsaver

Some clarinettists use a *padsaver*, a long fluffy plume which you stick into your clarinet after drying it. Others prefer not to: padsavers leave behind fibres which can stick to the pads and they often don't absorb the moisture but just spread it around – and they also have metal rods which can damage the bore. So a swab is better on all counts.

Side pocket

The best place to keep your swab is in a side-pocket of your case. If you store it in or very near to your clarinet, pads and springs can be affected by the moisture in the cloth.

Wait a while

If you can't easily take your clarinet apart after playing it, leave it for a quarter of an hour to let it cool down. If that doesn't help, don't use a wrench or undue force but wrap it carefully in a towel and take it to be repaired.

Locked

Put your clarinet back in its case in exactly the same way it was before you took it out. Some cases have lids which automatically click shut when you close the case. If yours doesn't, always make sure you close the lid properly before you pick up the case.

QUICK REMEDIES

Serious maintenance is covered in the next chapter, but here are some quick fixes to help you deal quickly with the minor and common problems that may interrupt your playing.

Rattling

If you suddenly hear a rattling noise when you are playing or a key fails to open, it's probably down to a damp or sticking pad. The pads of the C sharp/G sharp key and the trill keys are especially temperamental. You can sometimes solve the problem by blowing out the moisture or blowing it off from the outside.

Cigarette papers

If blowing doesn't do the trick, dirty pads can usually be cleaned with a cigarette paper or a special *pad cleaning paper*. Simply slide a paper between the pad and the tonehole and carefully hold the key closed for a little while. If you're using cigarette papers, make sure the gummed edge of the paper never touches the pad – you may want to tear this edge off just in case, or buy non-gummed papers if you can find them. If there's still no improvement, take a clean paper, drip a tiny amount of lighter fluid or alcohol-based cleaning fluid onto it and repeat the steps above. Dry the pad with a fresh cigarette paper afterwards. Be careful when using lighter fluid or alcohol: it's highly flammable.

Preferably not

It's better not to clean or dry pads with talcum powder or other kinds of powder, and avoid other kinds of paper too. If you have leather pads, you can use paper tissues to clean them.

Oil

The pad of the C sharp/G sharp key is especially prone to becoming waterlogged: when you play, the condensation that collects in the instrument tends to run down towards that key, which is at the bottom of the tube. Some technicians prevent the problem by carefully drawing a tiny line of oil alongside or around the tonehole in question. The idea is that the moisture will follow the oil and not end up in the tonehole, but you need to be very accurate: a pad could be ruined if you get oil onto it. It's probably best not to do this yourself.

Loose springs

If a key has stopped working, this may also be due to a spring which has come loose. It's often quite easy to put loose springs back into place. If the spring of a closed key is missing, you may be able to play on by holding the key shut with a elastic band. But always take the elastic band off after playing and don't store any in your case. Rubber contains substances which are harmful to silver – so don't keep erasers in your case for the same reason.

Loose tenons

Sometimes the cork on one or several of the tenons is so badly worn away that it suddenly stops gripping. A temporary solution is to twist a cigarette paper or some yarn around it. After you have finished playing, get it recorked as soon as possible.

SAFETY TIPS

A clarinet is a serious investment – they are expensive, and sometimes irreplaceable. Here are a few extra tips on keeping yours safe.

Taking a break

Whenever you have a break from playing, put the cap on the mouthpiece and make sure your clarinet can't get damaged. It may be best to put the instrument on a clarinet stand. That way it will take up hardly any space and no one can accidentally sit down or step on it.

Stands

You can buy a stand which folds up to a very small size for as little as £10. The longer the feet are, the less chance there is that someone will knock it over. On some stands, the cone that the clarinet slides onto is covered with felt, giving you optimum protection against scratches and wear to the bore.

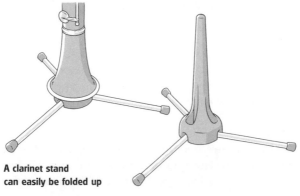

**A clarinet stand
can easily be folded up**

Avoid heat
Never leave a clarinet where it will get too hot or too dry. Watch out for heaters, radiators and other hotspots.

Insurance
Consider insuring your instrument. Depending on their value, musical instruments usually fall into the category of 'valuables' for home insurance. This means you have to let your insurance company know you have an instrument in order for it to be covered. Some home insurance policies also allow you to take out extra cover for your instrument to protect it when you take it out of the house. This can be quite expensive, but it means your clarinet will be covered against theft and damage, whether you're on the road, at a practice or on stage. Some insurance companies also do specific policies for musicians.

Serial number
Note down the serial number of your instrument, as it may be required by your insurance company or the police if the instrument is ever stolen or lost. There's a form to do this to do this on page 133. And keep hold of your proof of purchase.

On the road
If you're taking your clarinet out and about in a car, don't put it on the parcel shelf, where it may be exposed to lots of sunshine. Where possible don't leave the instrument in a parked car, and if this is necessary, be sure it's not visible from the window. If you're travelling by bus or train, try to avoid leaving your clarinet on the luggage rack, from where it could fall down or be stolen.

CASES AND BAGS
Every new clarinet comes with its own case or bag, but if you fancy something a bit more luxurious there is a huge selection to choose from.

Five parts
You can get cases and bags with two, four, five and seven compartments. The most common are the ones with five compartments, which the instrument fits into in five

parts: mouthpiece with cap and ligature, barrel, upper joint, lower joint and bell.

French-style

Hard-shell *French-style* cases are often used in combination with loose case bags or case covers. Other styles are rectangular and flat like a briefcase. Cases like these don't give away the fact that you're carrying a musical instrument, which is good for security (though they often look like cases for laptop computers which are just as attractive to thieves).

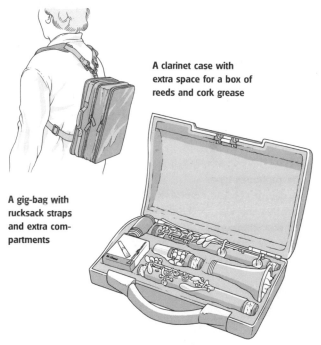

A clarinet case with extra space for a box of reeds and cork grease

A gig-bag with rucksack straps and extra compartments

Bags

As well as hard cases, there are various types of soft case around. *Gig-bags* are textile cases with soft, padded sides. They usually have an accessory pocket, a sheet music compartment, and adjustable rucksack straps that offer a safe way to transport a clarinet when biking or walking. Another option is a *carryall bag*. These have shoulder straps and lots of extra space which you can use for a music stand, sheet music and other bits and pieces, and also disguise the fact that you are carrying a musical instrument.

Space

If you're buying a new case, check out how much extra storage space it offers. Will you be able to fit a box of reeds and a reed guard in it, or a second mouthpiece, an extra barrel, cork grease, a neck strap or a special, detachable thumbrest? Does it have a side-pocket for your swab, a music stand or a lyre?

Prices

Separate cases and bags are on sale from around £20. If you want a luxury version in wood or leather and with space for a pair of clarinets (A and B flat), you can easily spend ten times that much.

MICROPHONES

If you want your clarinet to be louder than it is – if you're playing in a jazz club, for example – you'll have to use a microphone and amplification. Some players also use a microphone to allow them to put their instrument through various effects, or to record themselves playing.

Microphones types

A decent vocal microphone is fine for use with a clarinet, but there are also special clarinet systems available, with one or two small mikes that you clamp on to the instrument. Because these mikes only produce a very weak signal, they always come with a separate pre-amplifier, which you put

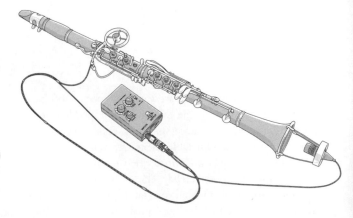

A small microphone with a special clamp (SD Systems)

in your pocket or attach to your belt. The signal then goes from the pre-amplifier, which usually has volume and tone controls, to the 'real' amplifier.

Movement or variation

A clip-on microphone gives you more freedom to move around than a vocal microphone on a stand. On the other hand, if your mike is on a stand, you can vary your volume and sound by changing the distance between it and your instrument.

Cordless systems

If you want total freedom to move around, you could even consider getting a cordless system, though these are much more expensive.

9. MAINTENANCE

If you make sure you do the kind of things mentioned in the previous chapter, your clarinet probably won't need much additional maintenance. A bit of extra cleaning now and again and perhaps the odd drop of oil should be all there is to it. Once in a while, though, your clarinet will need to be taken to a technician for an overhaul.

Ebonite mouthpieces should be cleaned now and then, preferably in lukewarm water. A special mouthpiece brush is useful for this. Remove chalk scale with a mouthpiece cleaner, which will also disinfect the mouthpiece. Don't leave ebonite and wooden mouthpieces to soak in water and avoid using vinegar or washing-up liquid if you want to keep them looking their best. Vinegar and washing-up liquid won't damage most other types of mouthpieces, though.

Polishing the keywork

A nickel-plated mechanism needs no more to shine it up than a wipe with a dry cloth. If you have a silver-plated mechanism, you can use a silver polishing cloth to clean it now and again. But don't do this too often or the built-in polishing agent will wear through your silver plate.

Not ordinary polish

Ordinary silver and metal polishes tend to be too abrasive for use on clarinet mechanisms. They can leave a residue that may get inside the keywork and make everything grow steadily stiffer, and they can also damage the pads. In other words, they're best avoided.

Blackened

If your silver-plated keywork tarnishes faster than you can polish it, you may be better off getting an instrument with a nickel-plated mechanism, or having the mechanism gold-plated. Rapid discoloration of silver can be caused by your sweat and exacerbated by something in your diet such as spinach or eggs and certain medicines, or it could be the fault of erasers or elastic bands in your case, a case whose lining was stuck down with the wrong kind of glue, or even a new ebonite mouthpiece. If your mouthpiece seems to be the guilty party, store it in a plastic bag outside the case for the first few weeks.

Oiling the mechanism

The best way to oil the mechanism is to take it apart completely – so it's best to leave the job to a technician. If only a few of the keys are stiff and you decide to do it yourself, use as little oil as possible. Dip a match or a pin into a little oil on a saucer or a piece of paper and then apply it to the hinge. Buy special oil from your music shop, not whatever you happen to have at home. Three tips: oil is disastrous for pads, so be very careful; chances are that you'll apply too much oil at once if you use an oil pen (a bottle with a hollow needle); and don't oil a mechanism that already works smoothly.

Cleaning

The best way to clean the little nooks and crannies of the mechanism is with a small brush or artist's paintbrush. The more often you do it, the less chance that dust and dirt will become lodged there.

Play

When you're polishing the mechanism, check for play, too. Play may simply be down to a loose screw, but it can also be caused by wear. It's best to get the instrument checked by a professional if you find anything amiss: the problem will only get worse.

Toneholes

Even if you always play with clean hands, the edges of the open toneholes will eventually become dirty. You can buy special sticks to clean them with, but ordinary cotton buds will do – as long as you make sure no strands of cotton end up inside the clarinet.

Rings

Now and then, check whether the bell ring, tenon rings and body rings are still tight. Loose rings can cause buzzes, and they also show that the wood has shrunk, indicating that the clarinet is being stored or has been stored in conditions which are too dry. Air conditioning and central heating systems are two of the main causes for dry air. An air humidity level of 40 to 60 percent is usually considered good for both musical instruments and people.

OILING THE BORE

There are few things clarinettists disagree about as strongly as oiling the bores of wooden clarinets. Some do it every three months, while others have been playing without oil (and without problems) for decades. Some factories recommend that you oil a new clarinet; others advise against it. The simplest advice is to ask when you buy your instrument, or to leave it to a technician.

Cracks

Most experts believe that a layer of oil in the bore reduces the risk of cracks. But others say that grenadilla is so hard that oil could never prevent a clarinet from cracking. The only thing that can be said for sure is that clarinets sometimes crack, whether or not they've been regularly oiled.

The best way

Oil hardly penetrates the wood, if at all, but leaves behind a thin, protective film. The best way to oil the bore is to first allow the instrument to dry thoroughly. Then remove the mechanism, oil the wood, clean the toneholes, reassemble the instrument and regulate it – a job for a professional, in other words.

Easier

The easiest way to oil the bore is to dry the instrument as well as you can, put pieces of clingfilm under all the pads, put a very small amount of oil on a special cleaning rod and move it backwards and forwards through the tube a few times. Never forget that it's easier to damage a clarinet by using too much oil than by using too little.

Almond oil and bore oil

The most common type of oil used is sweet almond oil, which you can buy from health food shops. Special bottles of *bore oil* are also available. The drawback of these types of oil is that they don't dry, so they easily get wiped off again.

Hard oil and wax

Linseed oil and tung oil do dry, which means they stay on the wood longer. These 'hard' oils are best applied by an expert, because if you use a bit too much you can end up with a crusty, gel-like layer inside your clarinet. Beeswax is sometimes used as an alternative to such oils.

SERVICE AND OVERHAULS

All new clarinets need to be completely checked and regulated after six months to a year. In some cases, that first service is included in the purchase price.

Cleaning, oiling and adjusting

If you get your clarinet checked once a year, you can be fairly sure that nothing major can go wrong. Some technicians consider once every two years to be sufficient, depending on how much you play. A basic service (cleaning, oiling and adjusting) usually costs between £25 and £40. The longer you wait, the more expensive it will get.

Overhaul

Every clarinet needs to be overhauled once every five to ten years. If you so desire you can have your instrument made as good as new, with new pads, new tenons, new silver plating, new springs, new rods, new screws – you name it. The price will mainly depend on what needs to be done, but also on the quality and age of the clarinet.

Regulation

When you take your instrument for a service or overhaul, the technician will regulate it for you. Try your instrument out before you take it home so that you know that all the rings and keys are properly regulated for the way you play.

10. BACK IN TIME

The clarinet is already three centuries old, perhaps even older, and it has ancestors going back thousands of years. So it's not surprising that historians disagree about many points in its development. This chapter provides a brief history of the clarinet, all the way from the ancient memet to the instrument used in concert halls today.

To find the very first predecessors of the clarinet you have to go back to ancient Egypt, where they were playing an instrument called a *memet* as long ago as 3000BC. This instrument had a reed cut from the tube itself, to which it was attached only on one side. This kind of instrument is known as an *idioglottic* instrument.

One tube or two

The clarinet had many other ancestors and early family members, such as the Greek *aulos*, the Chinese *cuen kan*, the ancient Arabian *arghul* and the Welsh *pibgorn*. These are all instruments with a single reed, and either one or two tubes.

Chalumeau

The *chalumeau* was another single-reed instrument. According to some experts, the chalumeau was already being played two thousand years ago, but others claim that it's more likely to have developed in the Middle Ages. Similarly, some books written by experts will tell you that not a single chalumeau has been preserved, while other, equally scholarly works display photographs.

Register key

The most important difference between the chalumeau and the first clarinets is the register key. Without a register key, the chalumeau had a range no larger than – you guessed it – the chalumeau register of the modern clarinet.

Clarinet

With the introduction of the register key, musicians were suddenly able to make the instrument sound a lot higher. This higher register in some ways resembled the sound of a trumpet, and so the clarinet got its name; the word clarinet is derived from the Italian words for trumpet, clarino, or small trumpet, clarinetto.

Denner and sons

It is unclear exactly who invented the register key, and hence the clarinet. But most sources agree that the a man called Denner was responsible. Some experts claim it was the Nuremberg instrument maker Johann Christian Denner; others say it must have been one of his sons, because the clarinet is first mentioned in 1710, three years after the death of the older Denner.

Five to six keys

Gradually the clarinet acquired more and more keys: without these extras it could only be played in tune in certain major or minor keys. Around 1800, most clarinets had around five or six keys.

Iwan Müller

In 1812, the clarinettist Iwan Müller produced a clarinet with thirteen keys, enough to be able to get by in any key.

Boxwood clarinet in C with five keys and ivory body rings
(Savary, Paris, 1780; J. Schaap collection)

Those thirteen keys were not the only innovations of Müller's: he also used a metal ligature and was one of the first clarinettists to turn the mouthpiece around, so that the reed was placed on the lower lip instead of the upper lip.

Bärmann and Oehler

Half a century later, Carl Bärmann added a further five or six keys to the Müller clarinet, and another half a century after that, Oskar Oehler used Bärmann's design as the basis for his own clarinet – which most German professionals still play today.

Albert and Sax

Improvements on Müller's work were being made in Belgium, too, by Eugène Albert (after whom the 'German' Albert system is named) among others. Another famous Belgian who occupied himself with clarinets was Adolphe Sax, who invented the 'sax-o-phone' around 1840.

Klosé and Buffet

Around the same time, the Frenchmen Hyacinthe Klosé and Louis Auguste Buffet were also working on the clarinet. Put simply, they took some of the ideas of Theobald Boehm, the inventor of the modern flute, and applied them to the clarinet. Boehm himself had nothing else to do with their clarinet, but the new system was nevertheless named after him.

The future

Since Albert, Oehler and the first Boehm clarinets, nothing much has changed. Some experts say that's a good thing, since they consider the modern clarinet to be a perfect instrument. Others feel the clarinet could do with a total reinvention, because all sorts of things need improving . . .

11. THE FAMILY

The immediate clarinet family consists of at least thirteen instruments in different pitches. But it's also related to all kinds of other instruments with single reeds, and if you include all the members of the woodwind family of instruments, you need to add the saxophone, flute, oboe and bassoon, among others.

Clarinets come in all kinds of sizes. The most popular is of course the soprano clarinet in B flat, followed by the soprano clarinet in A, but there are also smaller soprano clarinets in C, D and E flat. The E flat instrument is so much smaller that it doesn't usually have separate upper and lower joints.

Higher clarinets

Though they're very rare, some clarinets are even smaller and higher than the E flat instrument. These clarinets, which include the *sopranino* E and the high A flat, used to be found in many European wind bands.

Basset clarinet

All the other clarinets sound lower. One example is the *basset clarinet*, which is really an extra-long soprano clarinet in A. That extra length means the lowest note is a C, instead of the usual E. Mozart's famous clarinet concerto was in fact written for this instrument – which is why it is sometimes known as a *Mozart clarinet*.

Basset horn

The modern *basset horn*, which is pitched in F, most closely resembles an alto clarinet. The German version has the basset keys, which are operated with the right thumb, at the back of the instrument, while the French version has them at the front. Earlier basset horns came in many different models; one of them had a semi-circular tube, which explains the 'horn' part of its name.

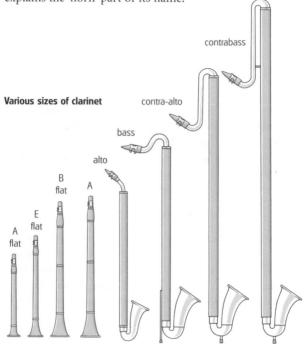

Various sizes of clarinet

contrabass

contra-alto

bass

alto

B flat

A

E flat

A flat

A flat

Contra-alto, contrabass and sub-contrabass

If you want to go lower still, you need a contra-alto clarinet (which sounds an octave lower than the alto clarinet) or a contrabass clarinet (an octave lower than the bass clarinet). Both come in a variety of models – some featuring a straight wooden, metal or plastic tube, others a coiled metal tube with two bows in it. The extra bows make these long instruments a bit shorter, so you can play them while sitting on an ordinary chair. And then there's the sub-contrabass clarinet: this very rare instrument goes another octave lower than the contrabass.

Harmony clarinets

Clarinets larger or smaller than the soprano are sometimes collectively called *harmony clarinets*: in many orchestras

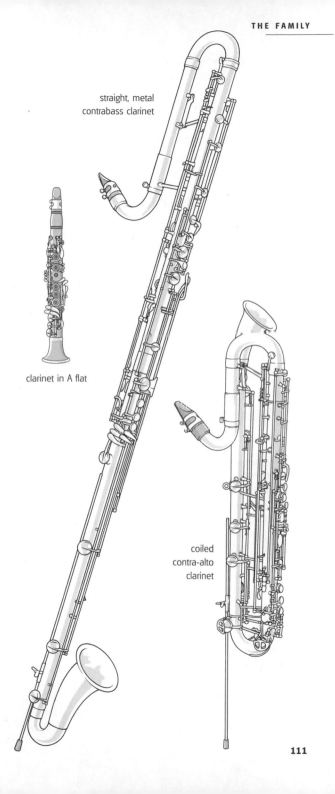

straight, metal
contrabass clarinet

clarinet in A flat

coiled
contra-alto
clarinet

and ensembles they're used to play the harmonies that accompany the soloist or the melody.

Turkish and Greek in G

There are many other varieties of clarinet. One example is the metal soprano clarinet in G which is much used in Turkish and Greek music.

Folk clarinets

Besides the immediate clarinet family, various countries and regions have their own *folk clarinets*. The most important thing they have in common is that they all have single reeds. Most of them have only five or six toneholes and no keys. One of the best-known is the wooden Hungarian *tárogató*, which most closely resembles a widely-flared clarinet, or, depending on how you look at it, a wooden soprano saxophone.

WOODWIND INSTRUMENTS

The clarinet belongs to the family of *woodwind* instruments, as opposed to *brasswind* family, which contains instruments like the trumpet and trombone. Here's a quick look at the other common members of woodwind family.

Saxophone

The saxophone is perhaps the instrument which is closest to the clarinet. The mouthpiece in particular looks the same, and the mechanism, too, has much in common with a clarinet's.

Conical

One major difference is that a saxophone is entirely conical: from the mouthpiece onwards it becomes steadily wider. This makes it sound different, and hence play differently. And if you open the register key or *octave key* of a saxophone, it sounds an octave higher, rather than the twelfth of the clarinet.

Flute

If you look only at the keywork, a flute looks a lot like a clarinet too. Hardly surprising, this, because the Boehm

A flute, an oboe, an alto saxophone and a soprano saxophone

clarinet mechanism is derived from the mechanism which
Theobald Boehm invented for the flute.

Air stream
A flute has no register key. You move up to a higher register
by varying the angle of your air stream, or *overblowing*.
When you overblow, you go up an octave.

Oboe and Bassoon
An oboe has a conical tube like a saxophone, and is made
of wood like a clarinet. Even so, it sounds very different to
both instruments, mainly because it has a completely
different type of reed: an oboe is a *double-reed instrument*,
and the sound is created by two reeds vibrating against
each other. Another common double-reed instrument is
the much larger bassoon.

113

STOPPED PIPE

The clarinet is the only woodwind instrument that goes up not eight notes (an octave) but twelve when you change register. This is because it has a mostly cylindrical tube, which is blocked at one end – by the mouthpiece. As a result, a clarinet behaves like a *stopped pipe*, in acoustic terms.

Three times as fast

In a stopped pipe, going up to the next register makes the air vibrate three times as fast. If you play a low E, for example, the air vibrates 165 times a second (165 hertz). If you then go to the next highest register, the air vibrates three times as fast again, at 495 hertz – sounding a high B.

Much lower

Stopped pipes sound a lot lower than you would expect from their length. For instance, a clarinet sounds almost an octave lower than a soprano saxophone, a flute and an oboe, although all four instruments are pretty much the same length.

Open or conical

In other words, flutes, oboes and saxophones don't behave like stopped organ pipes – flutes because they are open at both ends, and saxophones and oboes because they have conical, not cylindrical, bores. If you move up to the next register on those instruments, the air starts vibrating twice as fast, not three times as fast, which makes the pitch just one octave higher.

12. HOW THEY'RE MADE

Almost all clarinets are made in factories large or small. Of course, there are all kinds of differences between the methods used to make cheap and expensive instruments, but in very general terms, clarinets everywhere are built in the same way.

The material for wooden clarinets is delivered to the factory as square-ended blocks (*billets*): longer ones for the upper and lower joints, short ones for the barrels and big, almost square blocks for the bells. In order to prevent the wood from cracking later, it first needs to be thoroughly dried. Before the drying process begins, the square blocks are first turned on a lathe to cut them into a round shape,

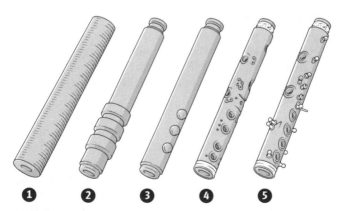

A lower joint in various stages of manufacture:
(1) pre-drilled, roughly turned and dried, (2) more finely machined, with bands for the chimneys and with tenons, (3 and 4) with chimneys, toneholes and holes for the mechanism drilled, and (5) with pillars

after which a hole is drilled lengthways down the middle. This will later become the bore.

Years or hours
The wood is sometimes still left to dry for years in the old-fashioned way. But in most factories this stage takes place in special kilns, which dry the wood much faster. More expensive clarinets are often made of older wood, which has the least risk of cracking.

Cut and drilled
After the wood has been dried, the inside and outside of the instrument are cut to size and drilled using various computer-controlled machines. The tubes of some clarinets, those which are to have integral toneholes (see page 37), are left with raised bands of wood on the outside. These are later cut into the chimneys for the ring key toneholes using a special lathe.

Moulds
The components of plastic clarinets are sometimes made in the same way but other, cheaper instruments are cast, which means they come out of the mould in their final shape. This technique usually allows less accuracy in determining the exact dimensions of the bore than using drills and lathes.

Polishing
The wooden components are extensively polished to make them mirror-smooth and shiny. Often they are then submerged in an oil bath for several days or even longer. To make coloured instruments, the oil may be mixed with Indian ink or another dye.

Pillars and mechanism
Once all the components are ready, the pillars and rings are attached, after which the mechanism is mounted. Before they leave the factory, the instruments are regulated and tested. The more expensive the instrument, the more attention is devoted to this testing stage. Indeed, more expensive instruments are often fine-tuned by hand, for example by very carefully reworking the toneholes and the bore.

REEDS AND MOUTHPIECES

Most reeds are made of *Arundo donax*, a type of cane which grows particularly well in Var in southern France, but also in South America, Australia and elsewhere.

Ripening

The plants are harvested when they are two to three years old. By then they have usually grown to about eight metres (25 feet) in height. After harvesting, the cane is allowed to dry for a year or more, during which time it develops a golden yellow colour.

By size and into shape

The stalks are then chopped into short pieces and sorted by size: thick sticks for the big reeds used on bass clarinets or large saxophones, thin ones for small E flat clarinets and so on. Afterwards, each round section is split into four or six pieces and shaped further by a whole series of machines: the reed is flattened, the facing polished, the profile made and the tip cut into its round shape. At each stage, the reeds are inspected visually and the bad ones are discarded.

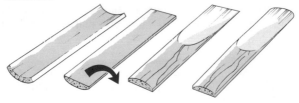

From cane to reed

Number

A separate device measures the stiffness of each reed. The stiffer the reed, the higher the number it is given. Next, the reeds are once again inspected thoroughly, then stamped and packed.

Mouthpieces

Most mouthpieces start life as small blocks of ebonite, glass, wood or metal, which are cut into shape by computer-controlled lathes. On more expensive mouthpieces, the shape of the facing is still finished by hand. The very cheapest plastic mouthpieces are cast in one go.

13. THE BRANDS

The number of clarinet manufacturers and brands is quite limited when compared to other instruments such as guitars or violins. A few large firms dominate much of the market, but there are also quite a few smaller manufacturers, many of which only produce clarinets in the higher price ranges.

The three main French clarinet manufacturers – Buffet-Crampon, Leblanc and Henri Selmer – are the biggest sellers worldwide. Another important name is the Japanese Yamaha brand, a company which also makes all kinds of other instruments.

 Buffet-Crampon was formed when Jean Louis Buffet, whose father had also been a clarinet maker, married Zoé Crampon in 1836. Besides clarinets in all price ranges, the French firm makes oboes and saxophones. The cheaper clarinet series are actually made by the German company Schreiber. Both Schreiber and Buffet-Crampon are owned by former English clarinet maker Boosey & Hawkes.

Leblanc is the best-known name of the company which also owns the brands Vito, Noblet and Holton. In 1904, the firm which flute and oboe maker Denis Noblet had founded in 1750 was taken over by Georges Leblanc, whose son Léon teamed up with the American Vito Pascucci in

1946. Only wooden clarinets in all price ranges built in France are sold under the name Leblanc. The Noblet brand name is used for a limited range of French-made wooden student instruments. The Vito and Holton names are mainly used for plastic clarinets made in the US.

Henri Selmer, solo clarinettist with the Paris Opéra Comique, started his firm in 1885. The French Selmer company makes all the popular sizes in the clarinet family, in both the professional and the mid-price ranges. Selmer has also long been the biggest brand for professional saxophonists. The company is independent of its American namesake, which is mainly known for its less expensive plastic instruments.

YAMAHA® The one-man organ factory founded by Torakusu Yamaha in 1889 is now the world's biggest producer of musical instruments, from B flat to bass clarinets in all price ranges, from drum sets to grand pianos, from trumpets and amplifiers to synthesizers – and Yamaha also makes motorbikes, hi-fi equipment, sailing boats and much more. Yamaha is still a Japanese company, but its instruments are built in different locations around the world.

OTHER BRANDS

A few other brand names you may come across include the Czech **Amati** brand (one of the few to still build Full-Boehm clarinets; see page 46), **Artley** and **Selmer** from the United States, **Hanson** from the UK, the Taiwanese **Dixon** and **Jupiter** brands, **Orsi** and **Ripamonti** from Italy and **Lark** from China. These brands are mainly active in the lower price range. You'll find the names of Jupiter and Dixon on all kinds of other instruments, too.

More expensive

There are also various brands that primarily produce clarinets in the higher price brackets – examples include British makers like **Eaton** and **Howarth**, the Italian company **Patricola** and the **Rossi** firm from Chile, whose product-line includes one-piece B flat clarinets.

GERMAN CLARINETS

Most German factories either largely or exclusively make clarinets with the German or Oehler system. A few of the better-known names are **Bernd Moosman**, **Richard Keilwerth**, **Arthur Uebel**, **Püchner**, **Schwenk & Seggelke** and **Schreiber**, which collaborates with Buffet-Crampon, and **Hammerschmidt**, which also makes Austrian clarinets, tárogatós and other woodwind instruments.

HERBERT WURLITZER

The best known German brand name is that of Herbert Wurlitzer. The founder himself died in 1989, but his firm still exists. Plenty of professional orchestras won't even let you audition if you don't have an instrument by this expensive brand. The clarinets made by Herbert's father and predecessor Fritz Wurlitzer are at least as celebrated, and Germany has several other clarinet makers with the same surname.

OLD BRAND NAMES

On older clarinets you may sometimes come across brand names from the past. Two examples are **Boosey & Hawkes**, the British firm which stopped making its own clarinets when it bought **Buffet-Crampon**, and the French **SML** (Strasser-Marigaux-Lemaire) brand, also known as **Marigaux**, which closed down in the late 1990s.

14. GROUPS AND ORCHESTRAS

There's a great deal of music written for solo clarinet, in all different styles. And there's nothing stopping you from playing music written for other instruments with similar ranges, such as the violin. But there's also a huge amount of music written for groups and ensembles containing clarinet. This chapter introduces a few of them.

Clarinettists play in wind bands, clarinet choirs, wind quintets, duos, trios, gypsy orchestras, Dixieland groups, jazz bands, symphony orchestras and all kinds of other ensembles. Let's have a look at these in turn.

Wind bands
The clarinet is perhaps the most important instrument in a concert band or wind band. These large orchestras of between 40 and 100 musicians consist of woodwind (clarinets, saxes, etc), brass (trumpets, trombones, etc) and percussion. They play all kinds of different styles of music, from classical works to arrangements of rock songs. Besides many B flat clarinettists, who often play the main tune, concert bands sometimes include E flat and bass clarinets.

Show bands
A show band is a large orchestra composed mainly of wind players and percussionists. Show bands perform while marching, often in the most complex patterns.

Symphony orchestras
A symphony orchestra consists of over fifty musicians, with a large string section (violin, viola, cello, double bass) as

well as brass, woodwind and percussion. Most symphony orchestras have between two and four clarinettists, nearly always on B flat or A clarinets, though some works do also call for the E flat or bass clarinet.

Concertos

Just like violinists, pianists and other musicians, clarinettists can also perform as soloists with orchestral accompaniments. Pieces for soloist and orchestra are generally known as *concertos*, and though you probably won't have an orchestra at your disposal, most of the great clarinet concertos are also available in arrangements for clarinet and piano, and you can also get CDs containing the orchestral accompaniment.

Chamber orchestras

Not all orchestras are the size of a symphony orchestra. Chamber orchestras, for instance, have around twenty to forty musicians, usually with just one clarinet.

Chamber music

There is a great deal of music, collectively called *chamber music*, written for smaller groups of instruments. Some combinations are very common – the standard wind quintet, for example, consists of clarinet with flute, oboe, bassoon and French horn. But music has been written for practically every combination of instruments, from duos for two clarinets to octets with clarinet and seven other instruments.

With strings

The sound of the clarinet blends well with string instruments, and there are many pieces written for such combinations. For example, Mozart, Weber and Brahms wrote famous pieces for clarinet and string quartet (two violins, viola and cello). Alternatively, the clarinet can simply take the place of one of the violins in a string quartet. That means playing with a second violinist, a viola player and a cellist. Similarly, an alto clarinet could take the part of the viola, and a bass clarinet replace the cello.

Modern classical

Classical music is not just old music – it's still being written today. Composers of contemporary or modern classical music for clarinet call for all kinds of 'strange' noises and special effects, such as playing two notes at once (*multiphonics*). The bass clarinet appears in much contemporary classical music, partly because it offers a wide range of unusual sounds.

ONLY CLARINETS

More and more groups are being formed which consist entirely of clarinettists – from duos, trios and quartets to groups of five, fifteen or fifty musicians or more.

Clarinet choir

These larger groups are known as *clarinet choirs*. They exist at many different levels, from amateur to professional, and play all kinds of styles: hits, folk music, works specially written for clarinet choirs, arrangements of works for concert bands and symphony orchestras and much more besides.

From large to small

The bigger a clarinet choir is, the more likely it will be to have its own conductor. The B flat clarinettists are always the biggest group. All kinds of other clarinets may be used in addition, from the small A flat to the contrabass.

AND MORE

As well as the groups described above, there are many other groups that specialize in a particular style of music. Clarinets are used in the folk music of many different countries and regions (the Czech Republic, the Balkans, Turkey and Greece among them), as they are in gypsy and klezmer groups, in world music bands and in groups which accompany voice choirs, singers and musicals.

Jazz

No Dixieland band is complete without a clarinettist, and you often find them in big bands too. The saxophone edged the clarinet out of the jazz scene in the 1940s, but in recent years the instrument has once again been gaining ground.

GLOSSARY AND INDEX

This glossary contains short definitions of all the clarinet-related terms used in this book. There are also some words you won't find in the previous pages but which you might well come across in magazines, catalogues and books. The numbers refer to the pages where the terms are used in this book.

12th key If you open the *12th key* or *register key* of a clarinet, the note you are playing goes up by a twelfth, taking you to the next register. See also: *Register, register key.*

17/6 *(7)* Most clarinets have seventeen keys and six rings.

A clarinet *(12, 49, 110)* Sounds a semitone lower than the B flat clarinet, and is used mainly in orchestral and chamber music.

Acute register See: *Register, register key.*

Albert clarinet *(50, 52, 108)* A clarinet with a German mechanism.

Altissimo register See: *Register, register key.*

Alto clarinet *(13, 14, 110)* Is slightly larger than a B flat clarinet and sounds slightly lower. It has a metal neck and an upward-pointing bell, just like a bass clarinet. Alto clarinets are pitched in E flat.

Articulated G sharp *(46)* Rare extra key which makes various trills easier to play.

Arundo donax *(117)* The cane from which clarinet reeds are made.

Auxiliary E flat lever *(45)* An extra lever that allows you to operate the A flat/E flat key with your left little finger, as well as with the right one. Also called *auxiliary E flat/A flat lever*.

Baffle *(63, 69)* A kind of step on the inside of the mouthpiece which makes the sound brighter and more direct.

Barrel *(4, 5, 29, 56, 72–74)* Joint which connects the mouthpiece and the upper joint. Has a major influence on the sound of a clarinet. When adjusting tuning, you either pull out or push in the barrel slightly. Also known as *tuning barrel* and *socket*.

Bass clarinet *(2, 13, 14, 31, 48, 123)* Sounds an octave lower than a soprano clarinet in B flat. See also: *Alto clarinet*.

Basset horn, basset clarinet *(109–110)* A basset horn (pitched in F) sounds just a little lower than an alto clarinet. A basset clarinet is a soprano clarinet in A which has been stretched slightly, so extending its range.

Bell *(5, 29, 34–36)* The widely flared end of the clarinet.

B flat clarinet *(3, 11–12)*

The most popular clarinet is the soprano clarinet in B flat: the fingering C gives a sounding B flat.

B flat, improved *(47–48)* All kinds of systems have been devised to make the B♭' sound better. Even so, most clarinettists opt to do without.

Boehm clarinet *(14, 45, 47, 53)* The Boehm clarinet or French clarinet is the type most used around the world. Its sound, mechanism, bore, mouthpiece and reed are different to those of German clarinets. See also: *German clarinet*.

Bore *(31–34, 51, 53, 58)* The dimensions and shape of the inside of the clarinet. The bore is one of the most important factors in determining a clarinet's sound, along with the bore of the mouthpiece *(69)* and the barrel *(73–74)*.

Bridge *(10–11)* Connection between the upper joint and the lower joint. Also called *bridge mechanism*, *link* or *correspondence*.

Cases and bags *(98–100)* No clarinet should be without one.

Chalumeau 1. See: *Register,*

register key. 2. Precursor of the clarinet *(106)*.

Chamber *(63, 64, 69)* Space behind the window of the mouthpiece.

Clarinet register See: *Register, register key.*

Closed hole keys *(13, 16, 46)* Keys with solid pad cups rather than rings, for instance on alto and bass clarinets. Also known as plateau-style keys.

Correspondence See: *Bridge.*

Dalbergia melanoxylon See: *Grenadilla.*

E flat clarinet *(12–13, 16, 23, 110)* A smaller, higher-sounding clarinet.

Embouchure *(15)* A French word used to describe how a player blows and how they use their lips, jaws and all the muscles around them.

Facing, facing length *(63, 67–68)* The term facing may describe the tip opening of a mouthpiece, the lay (curvature and length), or both. See also: *Lay.* The word facing is also used to indicate the part of the reed that is in contact with

the table of the mouthpiece *(69)*.

File cut See: *French file cut.*

Fingering chart *(7)* Fingering charts show you exactly which keys to use for which notes.

Fork B flat *(45–46)* An extra ring which offers an alternative fingering for the B flat.

French clarinet *(14)* Another name for the Boehm clarinet. See: *Boehm clarinet.*

French file cut *(79)* To make a reed a *French file cut*, an extra section at the end of the thick part is filed away in a straight line.

Full-Boehm *(47)* A rare clarinet with all kinds of extra keys.

German clarinet *(50–54, 71, 108)* German clarinets have a different bore and a different mechanism, mouthpiece *(64–65)* and reed *(79–80)* to French or Boehm clarinets. There are various systems, such as the fairly simple German or Albert system, and the Oehler system *(50*)*, mainly used by professional clarinettists. Reform-

Boehm clarinets have a German bore and a French mechanism. See also: *Boehm clarinet*.

Gig bag *(99)* Sturdy, lined soft-shell case.

Grenadilla *(30)* The most commonly used variety of wood for clarinets. Sometimes known as ebony, M'pingo or African Blackwood; its botanical name is Dalbergia Melanoxylon.

Insurance *(98)*.

Intonation *(54–55, 90–92)* The better the intonation of a clarinet is, the less you have to do to play it in tune. Clarinet are never perfectly in tune, though: you always need to correct certain notes.

Key cup See: *Pad cup*.

Key opening See: *Venting*.

Keys *(5–7, 10–11, 39, 42, 43, 45–49, 60, 107)* A clarinet has keys with pads and open *rings* or *ring keys*, which close toneholes further down the instrument.

Keywork See: *Mechanism*.

Klosé clarinet *(108)* Another name for the Boehm clarinet, invented by Hyacinthe Klosé.

Lay *(63)* The area where the mouthpiece curves away from the reed, from the tip of the reed to the point where the reed touches the mouthpiece. See also: *Facing length*.

Ligature *(75–76)* The special clamp that is used to attach the reed to the mouthpiece.

Link *(10)* See: *Bridge*.

Long-pipe notes, long-tube notes The notes you play with most or all of the keys closed, so that you use a long section of the clarinet tube. When all or most of the keys are open, you're playing *short-pipe* or *short-tube notes*.

Lyre *(11)* A special clamp which can be mounted onto a clarinet to hold sheet music. Lyres are very useful if you play in a marching band.

M'pingo See: *Grenadilla*.

Mechanism *(39–49)* The entire system of keys and rods which allows you to open and close all the toneholes. Also called the *keywork*.

Metal clarinet *(31)* Mainly used in folk music.

Mouthpiece cushion *(70–71)* A cushion made of a soft material which protects both mouthpiece and teeth.

Mouthpiece *(4, 5, 56, 61, 62–72, 117)* How you sound and play depends primarily on your mouthpiece and your reed.

Neck *(74)* Alto, bass and other large clarinets have a (metal) neck instead of a barrel. Also known as *crook* in the UK.

Neck strap *(16)* Takes the weight of the instrument off your thumb.

Nickel-plated See: *Silver-plated.*

Octave key See: *Register key.*

Oehler clarinet See: *German clarinet.*

Pad cup *(43)* The actual keys or 'lids' which stop the toneholes. Also known as *key cups.*

Pads *(10–11, 49, 59, 94, 95–96)* Small discs made of felt or cork, covered in (animal) membrane, leather or plastic, which seal the toneholes.

Plateau-style keys See: *Closed hole keys.*

Posts *(42)* The metal pillars with which the mechanism is attached to the clarinet.

Power-forged keys *(43)* Keys that are shaped by pressure, rather than cast. Sometimes advertised as a special feature, but virtually every clarinet has them.

Rails *(63, 68)* The tip rail and the side rails are the three edges of the window of a mouthpiece.

Reed *(4, 63, 65, 77–85, 88–89, 93–94)* Comparable to a string when you play the guitar or your vocal chords when you sing. Together with your mouthpiece, the reed is extremely important for the way in which you sound and play.

Reed cutter *(83)* Tool used to make reeds which are too light slightly shorter.

Reeds guard *(93–94)* Protective holder for reeds.

Reform-Boehm See: *German clarinet.*

Register, register key *(7–10, 48–49, 51, 52, 54, 59, 114)* The register key allows you to move from the low *chalumeau register* to the *clarinet register* or *clarino register* (also known as *clarion register*, *upper register* or *overblown register*). The third and highest register is called the *acute* or *altissimo register*. The register key is also known as the *speaker key*, *12th key* or, wrongly, the *octave key*.

Register tube *(37–38)* Small tube attached to the register key tonehole.

Rings, ring keys *(5, 45, 52)* See: *Keys*.

Rollers *(51)* The rollers between the little finger keys of German clarinets make it easier to move from one key to the other.

Secondhand buying tips *(25–26, 59–61)*

Short-pipe notes, short-tube notes *(55)* See: *Long-pipe notes, long-tube notes*.

Silver-plated *(22, 42, 102–103)* Clarinets either have silver-plated or nickel-plated mechanisms. Silver is more expensive and needs more maintenance; nickel looks a bit 'cheaper'.

Single cut See: *French file cut*.

Single-reed instruments *(106)* Clarinets are single-reed instruments, as are saxophones. Oboes and bassoons are double-reed instruments.

Socket See: *Barrel*.

Soprano clarinet *(3)* The most popular clarinet is the soprano clarinet in B flat. There are other soprano clarinets in C and A.

Speaker key See: *Register, register key*.

Speaker tube See: *Register tube*.

Stopped pipe *(114)* A cylindrical instrument which is blocked at one end behaves acoustically like a stopped pipe. The clarinet belongs to this group of instruments.

Tenons, tenon rings *(36, 94, 97)* The tenons are the cork-lined ends of each of the joints of a clarinet. Often they are reinforced with (metal) tenon rings

Thumb key See: *Register, register key*.

Thumbrest *(5, 41)* There are adjustable and non-adjustable thumbrests, and special thumbrests designed to avoid pain and discomfort.

Tip opening *(63, 66–67)* The distance between the tip of your reed and the tip of your mouthpiece.

Toneholes *(4, 36–39)* The holes in your clarinet. They are often *undercut*, which means that each hole gets slightly wider on the inside.

Transposing *(12–13)* Clarinets are transposing instruments, which means that the fingering you play has a different name to the note produced. The only non-transposing clarinet is the rare C clarinet.

Trill keys *(43–44)* Only the upper two of the four keys which you play with the side of your right hand index finger are actually designed for playing trills, but often all of them are referred to as *trill keys*.

Tuning *(38–39, 54–55, 92)* You tune a clarinet by pulling two or more joints apart slightly, or by using a different tuning barrel.

Tuning barrel See: *Barrel.*

Tuning ring *(92)* A thin ring which fills up the grooves on the inside of a clarinet which are formed when you pull apart the joints for tuning.

Undercut toneholes See: *Toneholes.*

Upper register See: *Register, register key.*

Venting *(55)* Exactly how far the closed keys open when you press them. This affects the sound of an instrument, and also its intonation. Also called 'key opening'.

Window *(63, 64)* The opening of the mouthpiece.

WANT TO KNOW MORE?

This book contains all the essential information about purchasing, understanding and maintaining clarinets, but if you want to known more there are many magazines, books and Websites you could turn to. This chapter suggests some of the best.

MAGAZINES

Though they may not be on the shelves of your local newsagent, there are a few magazines devoted to clarinets and clarinet playing. These are usually produced by organizations and societies – contact the society if you wish to subscribe.

- *Clarinet & Saxophone* (UK), 020 8979 6064, www.cassgb.co.uk
- *The Clarinet* (US), 001 630 665 3602, www.clarinet.org
- *Windplayer* (US), 001 310 456 5813, www.windplayer.com

BOOKS

Countless books have been written about clarinets and clarinettists. The books listed below cover the instrument itself and discuss other subjects such as technique, history and repertoire at greater length.

- *Clarinet*, Jack Brymer (Yehudi Menuhin Music Guides, Kahn & Averill, UK, 1976; 259 pages; ISBN 1 871082 12 9).
- *Cambridge Companion to the Clarinet*, Colin Lawson (Cambridge University Press, 1995; 240 pages; ISBN 470066 8/2).
- *The Clarinet and Clarinet Playing*, David Pino (Dover Publications, New York, 1980; 306 pages; ISBN 0-486-40270-3).

- *Clarinet Acoustics*, O. Lee Gibson (Indiana University Press, USA, 1994/1998; 84 pages; ISBN 0-253-21172-7).
- No longer for sale, but still to be found in libraries is *The Clarinet: Some Notes on its History & Construction*, F. Geoffrey Rendall; edition revised by Philip Bate (Ernest Benn Ltd., London, 1971; 206 pages; ISBN 0510-36701-1).

Reeds

Separate books have also been written about making and adjusting reeds. One example is *Making Clarinet Reeds by Hand* by Walter Grabner, which can only be ordered from the author's Website (www.clarinetXpress.com).

THE INTERNET

On the Internet you can find countless sites for clarinettists, often with all kinds of links, articles, discussion groups and answers to FAQs (Frequently Asked Questions). Two good sites with a lot of information and links are *The Online Clarinet Resource* (www.ocr.sneezy.org) and *The Clarinet Pages* (www.sneezy.org/clarinet). You could also try the Websites of clarinet societies such as the International Clarinet Association (www.clarinet.org).

Finding a teacher

If you're looking for a teacher, there are various organizations that may be able to help you. Try, for example: the Clarinet and Saxophone Society of Great Britain (www.cassgb.co.uk), the Musicians' Union (www.musicians union.org.uk), the Incorporated Society of Musicians (www.ism.org), the Federation of Music Services (http://fp.federationmusic.f9.co.uk).

ESSENTIAL DATA

In the event that your instrument is stolen or lost or if you just decide to sell it, it's always useful to have all the relevant data, such as the serial number and original purchase price, close to hand. You can jot down all these details on the following pages.

INSURANCE

Company:

Phone: Fax:

Email:

Agent:

Phone: Fax:

Email:

Policy number: Premium:

INSTRUMENTS AND ACCESSORIES

Brand and type:

Serial number:

Price:

Date of purchase:

Purchased from:

Phone: Fax:

Email:

Brand and type:

Serial number:

Price:

Date of purchase:

Purchased from:

Phone: Fax:

Email:

MOUTHPIECES

Brand and type:

Price:

Date of purchase:

Purchased from:

Phone: Fax:

Email:

Brand and type:

Price:

Date of purchase:

Purchased from:

Phone: Fax:

REEDS

Brand, type and number:

Price:

Comments:

Brand, type and number:

Price:

Comments:

Brand, type and number:

Price:

Comments:

ADDITIONAL NOTES

....

....

....

....

....

....

....

....

MUSIC ROUGH GUIDES ON C.

'Like the useful Rough Guide travel books and television shows, these discs delve right into the heart and soul of the region they explore'
— *Rhythm Music (USA)*